THE NEW ECONOMIC MENACE TO INDIA

THE NEW ECONOMIC MENACE TO INDIA

BY

BIPIN CHANDRA PAL

GYAN

Published by

Gyan Publishing House
5, Ansari Road
Daryaganj, New Delhi-110002
Phone: 011-47034999, 9811692060
E-mail: books@gyanbooks.com

Distribution Network
gyanbooks.com
India, USA, Canada, UK, Australia, France

ISBN: 978-81-212-8238-3 (PB)
First Published, 1920

2nd Impression 2023

Printed at: Gyan Press, Delhi.

THE NEW ECONOMIC MENACE TO INDIA
Author: BIPIN CHANDRA PAL

THE NEW ECONOMIC MENACE TO INDIA

THE NEW ECONOMIC MENACE TO INDIA

BY

BIPIN CHANDRA PAL

MADRAS

GANESH & CO.

1920

Contents

CONTENTS

CONTENTS

"In my own country in India, it is impossible to predict what effect the war will have. England will undoubtedly be sorely crushed in her material resources, no matter which way the war will end; and nations pressed for means often become more oppressive and exacting on their dependencies."

RABINDRA NATH TAGORE

in an interview

to the San Francisco California Examiner.

THE NEW ECONOMIC MENACE TO INDIA

I

QUESTION OF IMPERIAL FEDERATION

WE are afraid sufficient attention is not being paid by our active politicians to the great economic menace with which we are threatened by the new economic policy of the Empire, and the vigorous attempts that will be made presently for the exploitation of our material resources for the benefit of the British capitalist and profiteering classes. This had long been coming, though we did not take sufficient note of it here; and the late war has brought this thing to the very forefront of Imperial problems.

Ever since the awakening of political consciousness in the country, following in the wake of the new illumination emanating from our English schools and universities, our educated countrymen have been exclusively concerned with the problem of India's political freedom and have paid little attention to the more fatal processes of economic serfdom that have been going on with the influx of foreign, and particularly British capital into the country, and the so-called development of our economic resources by foreign, and specially British industrial and commercial enterprise. We have no doubt raised our protest against the fatal economic drain resulting from British rule. But the Indian public did not realise for a long time that British exploitation, far more than British administration, was the real cause of this economic drain. Owing to the obsession of this political idea when we heard of After-War

Imperial Reconstruction on all sides, we were innocently led to hope that this Reconstruction would lift India from her position of a dependent to that of an equal partner in the Empire. The announcement of August 20, 1917, helped very materially to strengthen this political obsession and articulate Indian opinion acclaimed this announcement as the promise of Indians coming political freedom, and commenced to concentrate itself upon the best and quickest way to the realisation of full responsible government in India.

Whatever excuse there might have existed in the early days of the war for setting an exaggerated value upon the talk of After-War Imperial Reconstruction, in which every British and Imperial statesmen indulged, after the meeting of the Imperial Conference in 1917, there was absolutely no justification for it. Because, at this Conference, at which two nominees of the

Government of India, the Maharaja of Bikaneer and Sir Satyendra Prasanna Sinha were present, definitely left the question of political or constitutional reconstruction of the Empire for future, leisurely settlement. All that the Conference did was to lay down certain broad principles that should regulate the course of Imperial policy and evolution. These principles were formulated in the official statement of the decisions of the Conference in the following terms :—

1. The full recognition of the Dominions as autonomous nations of the Imperial Commonwealth ;
2. The recognition of India as an important part of the Imperial Commonwealth ;
3. The recognition of the right of the dominions and of India to an adequate voice in the foreign policy and foreign relations ;

4. The working out of effective arrangements for continuous consultations on all important matters of common imperial interests and for such concerted action, founded on consultation, as the several Governments determine.

In plain English, this meant that the Government of India (which is not representative of, nor responsible to, the people of India, but which is subject to the authority of the British Cabinet and the British Parliament, and is, therefore, the custodians, primarily, of British interests in this country) and which had hitherto no place or voice in the determination of Imperial policy would henceforth have a place in the Imperial Conference or Cabinet along with the Dominion Governments. This would give to Great Britain two additional seats in this Cabinet to protect special British interests as against the interests of the

Dominions, if these should ever come in conflict with each other. The recognition given to India here was really the recognition of her status as a Dependency of Great Britain, if not, indeed, of the whole of the self-governing group of the Empire. The statement made in Parliament by Mr. Lloyd George rendered this meaning absolutely clear. He said: "In the constitution of the Empire, the Imperial War Cabinet would consist of the British Premier and such of his colleagues as dealt with Imperial affairs, and Dominion Premiers or special representatives, and an Indian representative appointed by the Government of India."

"It was hoped," the Premier added, "that this annual meeting (of the Imperial Conference) would become an accepted convention of the British constitution. In its present form the institution was elastic. They had not attempted to settle what constitutional developments this might lead to." "The whole question of constitutional reconstruction of the Empire was reserved for future consideration."

The reason of it is also very plain. In the first place, Great Britain herself is not very keen about it. While she is undoubtedly anxious to draw the self-governing dominions into closer association with her in the common business of the Empire, she is not as yet seriously prepared to bind herself to these dominions with any definite constitutional ties.

As for the Colonies, these are practically sovereign states, recognised as such in all practical affairs even by the "mother" country. The freedom which they enjoy under the existing loose relationship with the British Sovereign and the British Parliament, is considered by large numbers of Dominion statesmen as more convenient than the limitations which a well-defined federal constitution would impose upon them. The ideal of Imperial Federation, first propounded by Joseph Chamberlain immediately after the Boer war eighteen years ago, has not, therefore, "caught on." Great Britain herself has not as yet favoured it. A resolution brought by the New Zealand Premier before the Colonial Conference in 1911 was stoutly opposed by Mr. Asquith and had to be finally withdrawn. Mr. Asquith's opposition was due to the fear that in the Council of the Empire, which was proposed to be set up as the symbol and instrument of Imperial unity and authority, the representatives of the Mother Country would be swamped by those of the Overseas Dominions. Many of the Dominions also, on the other hand, have been increasingly conscious of the almost endless possibilities that lie before them. The smallest of these Dominions, Newfoundland and New Zealand, have an area about the size of the United Kingdom.

South Africa is about four times and Canada and Australia about thirty times the size of the British Isles. The incidence of revenue per head in the United Kingdom is £4—2*s*. compared to £4 in Australia, £3—6*s*. in Canada, £3 in Newfoundland, £2—17*s*. in South Africa, and £10—9*s*. in New Zealand. The incidence of trade (exclusive of imports that are re-exported is £22—16*s*. in the United Kingdom; £24—3*s*. in Canada; £20 in Newfoundland; £15—13*s*. in South Africa; £29—8*s*. in Australia; and £35 in New Zealand. The only thing in which the Dominions lack is man-power. But they have a higher birth-rate and a lower death-rate than the "Mother Country."* Unless something

*	Birth-rate.	Death-rate.
United Kingdom	23.9	14.2
Canada	27.82	15.12
Newfoundland	28.8	10.6
Australia	27.7	10.5
New Zealand	26.3	9.5

very unexpected and extraordinary happens to the modern world, the overseas Dominions of Britain will soon attain the position of the dominant countries of the world. They are fully conscious of it. The Dominions are, therefore, unwilling to commit themselves definitely to any relations or adopt any policy that might complicate or jeopardise their future development in any way. It is only natural, therefore, that they have not been prepared to accept any scheme of Imperial Federation with alacrity or enthusiasm.

And the main difficulty here has been India. What is to be the position of India in the federated British Empire ? This problem has staggered both British and Colonial statesmanship. Federation is possible only among states occupying the same status. The different members of the American Union were all self-governing states when the present federal constitution brought and knit them together into an organic whole. The self-governing members of the British Empire may be similarly federated without any difficulty. All that will have to be done to work up this federation, is for the British Parliament to transfer its present Imperial authority and functions to a Federal Council of the Empire on which both the United Kingdom and the overseas Dominions will be equally represented. But neither India nor Egypt nor the Crown Colonies can be admitted into this Federation upon the same terms. The overseas Dominions may be represented on the Council of the Empire, either indirectly through the nominees of their respective Parliaments or Cabinets, or directly by deputies elected by constituencies. The members of the Colonial Conferences which were started evidently as an experiment in an informal sort of federalism, have been elected by the Colonial Governments. In fact, practically, these Conferences have been conferences of Colonial Premiers. Upon the outbreak of the last war, these Conferences were enlarged and modified. Colonial representatives were invited to the Imperial War Cabinet to jointly discuss and deliberate upon the problems of war, with the British Premier and his colleagues. They were accepted, for the time being, as members of the Imperial Cabinet; and Mr. Lloyd George did not conceal it that he was here practically inaugurating the future Federal Council of the Empire.

In this Mr. Lloyd George introduced no revolutionary innovation, not even in inviting two Indian public men to join the Imperial Cabinet. In giving a place to these *nominees* of the Indian Government in the Imperial war cabinet, the British Prime Minister simply followed the principle of the old Colonial Conferences, in which the Colonies were represented by the nominees of the Colonial Governments. The precedent thus established by Mr. Lloyd George has not, therefore, created any new constitutional ties. It has simply raised the old Colonial Conference from the position of a Colonial to that of an Imperial Institution; and, in doing so, the Prime Minister quite logically made room in it for the *nominees* of the Government of India. This has tacitly accepted the right of the Indian Government, which is only a department of His Majesty's Government of the United Kingdom, (and which is at present in no way representative of, or responsible to, the Indian people), to equal constitutional status in the British Commonwealth of Nations, with that of the Dominion Governments.

II

THE COMPOSITION OF THE BRITISH EMPIRE

TO understand the grave meaning of this move, one must clearly realise the nature of the very complex problem that has been claiming the attention of Imperial statesmanship for the last twenty years, ever since the close of the Boer War and the promulgation of the federal idea by Mr. Joseph Chamberlain. This problem was presented, almost with savage candour, by the "*Times*" in an article published in its special Empire-Day Supplement on May 24, 1909.

At the very outset, the writer condemned the confusion of thought that prevailed in regard to the real nature and constitution of the British Empire, which, he said, is not a unity but a duality. The British Empire is not one homogeneous unit, but a union of different units with different characters and constitutions. These fall into two main divisions, according to Lord Milner, whose authority is quoted by the "*Times*", namely :—

i. The Self-governing Empire, including the United Kingdom ;

ii. The Dependent Empire, including India and all the Crown Colonies and Protectorates.

And this dual character of the British Empire must not be overlooked by those who desire to understand the real nature of the Imperial problem, as it is apprehended by present-day British Imperialism.

These two divisions of the British Empire stand not only apart from, but in many respects in contradiction to, each other. They have really nothing in common between them, except the authority of the British King and the British Parliament, to which both are subject. But even this subjection varies in degree and differs in nature, as between the self-governing and the dependent Empire. The sovereign head of the state is "king" in the self-governing Empire, and "Emperor" in India. These two terms connote that while he is a constitutional monarch in his relations with the former, he is an absolute monarch in relation to India. In fact, however, the British Sovereign has to act according to the advice of his ministers and the decisions of the Parliament in his capacity of both King and Emperor. This Parliament has absolute authority over the Government of India which is responsible to it for its acts and policy. But it has practically no authority, except in a few matters concerning inter-colonial legislation and foreign relations and questions of peace and war, over the Colonial Governments which are responsible to the people of the Colonies only.

Political and constitutional values in the self-governing and the dependent Empire not only differ widely, but are even mutually destructive.

The same divergence and opposition exists also in the social and moral values of these two parts of the British Empire. The self-governing group has a common civilisation, a common social economy, a common religion, and a common outlook upon life, which are fundamentally different from the civilisation, the social economy, the religion and general world-view of the peoples of the dependent group. Such fundamentally divergent and conflicting elements cannot be welded together into any sort of organic unity. In any case, Imperial statesmanship has not as yet given any evidence of its insight into, or appreciation of, those higher principles of social evolution and those higher ideals of Universal Humanity with which Indian, and particularly Hindu, culture has long been familiar, and which alone could furnish the basis of a real and permanent synthesis between these divergent and conflicting elements.

The conflicts inside the different groups constituting the British Empire are essentially conflicts of narrow and isolated national life and interests. This conflict, though obviously far more keen and vital as between the white and the non-white groups in the Empire, is not altogether absent even among the white members of the Imperial family themselves. The lessons of the American War of Independence, have no doubt taught Great Britain the wisdom of dealing with infinite tact and consideration with her white Colonies, and treat them practically as sovereign states, in any case, in all matters pertaining to their internal administration. But still the conflicts of national interests, particularly in economic and industrial matters, between the Dominions and the Mother Country have not as yet been settled. The consciousness of isolated national interests and the apprehension of possible divergence of ideals and conflicts of policy in the Colonial mind had been clearly brought out in the determination of both Canada and Australia to build their own navies and keep them under their own control, instead of making adequate money-contributions to the "Mother" Country and entrust her with the entire responsibility of protecting their sea-boards against foreign aggression, as was wanted by the British Government. The refusal of Canada to permit unrestricted and indiscriminate immigration from the "Mother" Country, without due regard to the needs of her own State and the interests of her existing population, as well as the commercial treaty which she proposed to form with the United States a few years ago, without consulting the British Government or considering the commercial interests of the British nation,—are manifest proofs of the conceit of isolated national interests in that Colony, which have not yet been reconciled, under any larger social or political formula or ideal, with those of the United Kingdom and the other parts of the Empire. Empirical statesmanship has been trying to keep down these elements of disruption inside even the white group of what the *Times* calls, the self-governing section of the Empire, by appealing to that very conceit of isolated national self-interests of the Dominions which constitute such a vital menace to the future unity and integrity of the Imperial Association.

III

EMPIRICAL IMPERIALISM

THIS downright Imperial empiricism has no solution to offer to the real problem of the Empire, the problem namely, How to work out a real and permanent reconciliation between the conflicts of interests and cultures in the conglomeration of countries and peoples constituting the present British Empire. On the contrary, this empiricism, if it is allowed to dictate Imperial policy, will be bound to contribute very materially to the complications of the Imperial problem, and may even ultimately force the premature and violent break-up of the Imperial organisation.

This downright Imperial empiricism has found its ablest and most authoritative exponent in the *Times*-Milner School of British Imperialists. This school frankly recognises the conflicts and complexities of the Imperial problem. These are due to the existence of "two very distinct and in some respects almost contrary conceptions, subordinate to the more general idea of maintaining the existence and prosperity of the Empire as a whole."

> "On the one side we have the Imperialism which looks mainly to the depending Empire, the Imperialist whose pride is in the extent of British Dominion, in the justice of British rule, in the mission of our people to take up the "white man's burden" and devote itself to the elevation of less advanced races. On the other we have the Imperialism whose main object is the closer organic union of the self-governing Dominions with the Mother Country and with each other in an equal

partnership, the Imperialist whose aim is to keep the growing democracies of the younger nations within the Empire by admitting them to an equal share in all those privileges and responsibilities of Imperial power which at present rest exclusively with the citizens of the United Kingdom. Imperialism in this sense is a purely democratic movement, a constructive policy working through the ordinary channels of politics in free communities, essentially of the same character as the movements, which, in the past, federated the American States after the Revolution, and which created the Dominion of Canada 40 years ago or the Australian Commonwealth in the last decade, or the movement which is on the eve of successfully uniting South Africa at the present moment (1909). Imperialism in the other sense tends, on the contrary, to be autocratic, to lay stress on administrative efficiency, to look with suspicion on a democratic system which it knows to be unsuited to the conditions of half the Empire, and with the least favourable side of which it is from time to time brought into contact."

IV

THE SOLUTION OF THE TIMES-MILNER SCHOOL

THE *Times*-Milner School of Imperialism, while frankly recognising the divergence and even the mutual opposition of these two ideas, does not, however, regard them as really incompatible. On the contrary, the self-governing Empire and the dependent Empire are considered to be "each essential to the other." Consequently that which justifies the closer constitutional union and co-partnership between the members of the self-governing group, including the Colonies and the United Kingdom, equally justifies the maintenance of the dependent group, including India and Egypt.

This "essential justification of the desire

for a permanent constitutional union of the various self-governing communities of the Empire" is:—

i. the sense of the kindred, the pride in a common type of civilisation;

ii. the consideration that "the break-up of the Empire would mean loss of kinship, estrangement, possibly even conflict"; and the consequent "danger and difficulty to the national life of each part from the aggression, economic or military, of Foreign Powers,—and in that category would inevitably be included the States that had at one time been united under the British flag"; and

iii. the consideration that the constitutional union of the self-governing communities of the Empire would mean, mutual peace, greater power for *defence against conflicting civi-*

> *lisations and economic co-operation.* (The Italics are mine).

But can the maintenance of the dependent Empire (*i.e.*, India, the Crown Colonies and the Protectorates) be justified on the same grounds? The *Times* admits that racial kinship, the desire to maintain a common civilisation do not demand the maintenance of the Dependent Empire; but "even here there is something akin to these grounds for union." *For the Dependent Empire offers a large field for the propagation of British ideas, and institutions, and the working out of the problems of modern civilisation among alien and less civilised peoples.* (The Italics are mine).

> "The system of government in the dependent Empire, though differing from that prevailing in the self-governing Empire, is still essentially British in its chief characteristics; the ultimate ideals our administrators set before

themselves, the type of civilisation they wish to work up to, are British no less; the dispute between them and their democratic critics in this country is one as to the time and the means, not as to the end. Severence of the Dependent Empire would mean a great destruction of British civilisation in the present and the cutting off of a great hope of its development in the future, and *if there cannot be any sense of racial kinship, there can grow in its place the consciousness of a common citizenship, and the pride in the greatness of inheritance common to members of the Empire whatever their race or form of government.*" (The Italics are mine).

But higher ethical and humanitarian considerations apart, the maintenance of the Dependent Empire is absolutely necessary for the very life of the self-governing

Empire. The Dependent Empire must be maintained for two reasons, one military and the other economic. From the military point of view, the "population and resources of the Dependent Empire, represent (i) positively, a direct addition to the defensive strength of the Empire as a whole; and (ii) negatively, it takes away from the potential military resources of the rivals and possible enemies of the Empire. From the economic standpoint, the Dependent Empire affords (i) a great market for Imperial industries, and (ii) an almost unlimited source of supply of raw materials for these industries. "*From the economic point of view, the Dependent Empire, which is also the tropical Empire, is an essential and indispensable correlative to the self-governing Empire which lies almost wholly in the temperate zone.*" (The Italics are mine).

"At present it is mainly the United

Kingdom which profits by this integral connection between its industries and the raw materials and consuming power of its tropical dependencies. But the other self-governing States of the Empire are rapidly passing from the purely agricultural to the industrial state, and as that process develops, will become increasingly conscious of the value of *the Dependent Empire, which, indeed, is in many respects the biggest asset which the United Kingdom will contribute to the common stock when it enters into real partnership with them.*" (The Italics are mine).

From another point of view also the Dependent Empire is of very great value to the self-governing Empire. For "*the administration of the Dependent Empire not only provides a career for thousands of Englishmen to-day, but creates a class of men whose official experience and high standard of public duty are undoubtedly an addition to our (i.e. English) national life.*" And here too, the *Times* says "*partnership in the Empire has something to offer to junior States, something well worth acquiring.*" (The Italics are mine).

But the *Times* has something to offer even to the Dependent Empire. This will be benefited by the closer and organic union of the self-governing Empire in two ways; (i) in regard to security against external aggression, and (ii) in regard to its economic development also.

> "Imperial rule means for the dependencies security against external aggression, freedom from domestic anarchy and oppression, the development of their resources, a market for their products and a steady progress towards a higher civilisation. The union of the self-governing Empire would in no way lessen these advan-

tages. It will furnish the military and naval protection which England alone cannot furnish indefinitely. It will provide the tropical regions of the Empire with an ever-increasing market in the temperate zone."

And in this community of interests, the *Times*-Milner School of Imperialism recognises the great principle and motive which will, or ought to, unite and keep together the two parts of the present British Empire. For, the self-governing Empire and the dependent Empire are each essential to the other. The constitutional union of the self-governing Empire, so far from prejudicing the Dependent Empire will improve its position, defensive, economic, and political. The maintenance of the Dependent Empire, *its development to its highest economic capacity, its contentment, its political progress, are of vital interest to the future of every part of the self-governing*

Empire." (The Italics are mine). And in view of this mutual inter-dependence of the two Empires, the two views of the Empire, namely, that which considers the self-governing members of it only, and that which considers the Dependencies alone, cannot be said to be antagonistic, but are only " complementary."

> " They are the component factors in a higher Imperialism which transcends each, and which represents the most stupendous synthesis of the human race ever attempted. The development and integration of the British Empire is the only practical and rational attempt at building up the Brotherhood of man which the next few centuries are likely to see."

V

THE DOUBLE TASK BEFORE BRITISH IMPERIALISM

BUT this ambitious peroration notwithstanding, the only principle of reconciliation, the only formula of this "stupendous synthesis" which the imagination of the "*Times*-Milner" school of Imperialism has been able to discover, is in the recognition of its "double task"—

(i) *"of strengthening and uniting the governing portion of the Empire,"* and

(ii) *"of developing and helping forward the governed."*

And it draws two practical corollaries from these conclusions.

First, a clear differentiation between the two problems involved in the *union* of the self-governing Empire and in the development of the dependent Empire; and

Second, the substitution of the partner-States as a whole for the United Kingdom, as the power directly controlling the affairs of the Dependent Empire.

But as this latter will take time, and must wait for further constitutional development, the way towards it can be prepared in several directions.

" In the first place, preferential trade relations between the Dominions and the Crown Colonies and India can do much to awaken the consciousness of mutual interest and to increase on the part of the Dominions, the knowledge of the nature of the inheritance which they are to administer in the future."

In the second place, " an effort should be made to enlist the energy and ability of the growing manhood of the Dominions in the government of the dependent Empire."

"At present that administration is open to them in theory. But in practice the opportunity is very limited. The way into the Indian Civil Service is made easy and smooth for the young Englishmen. The examination has been intentionally adapted to the ordinary Oxford or Cambridge course, so that he can make up his mind to compete at the last moment. The examination itself is held within two hours' journey of his University. It is absurd to say that the Canadian or Australian youth has the same opportunities, unless he cuts himself off from the ordinary studies of his country and comes over at a great expense to study in England. The Rhodes Scholarships may help to surmount the difficulty, but the only really satisfactory method is to allot so many places to each of the Dominions and to hold examinations locally or accept the nominations of the local University authorities."

Finally,—and this is the most significant item in the programme of this school of

Imperialism,—the old policy of *laissez faire* must be definitely abandoned in the administration of the Dependent Empire, the chief idea of which has hitherto been, to preserve order, and impose (?) justice, trusting to individual enterprise to bring about economic progress. Such a policy is no longer possible.

> "*A positive policy of development*, by preferences, by bounties, by steamship subsidies, by the vigorous building of railways, by well-equipped agricultural and forestry and mining department, must be carried out if the Dependent Empire is to play its proper part in the whole economic and defensive scheme, and if it is to be fit for any degree of political progress. The latter can only come by gradual stages, and on lines suited to the peculiar conditions of each part, and not by the hasty application of principles only workable

under entirely different circumstances. The rapid extension of self-government to the communities of British race was only possible because each individual contained in himself the whole political system which it had taken centuries to build up in Great Britain. Its extension in the Dependent Empire must not only be gradual, but must follow the inherent bent of the particular community, and can only approximate satisfactorily to the British type as the mind of the community itself approximates to that type."

In the meantime, however, British and Dominions Imperialists must apply themselves to the double task of :—

(1) "strengthening and uniting the governing portion of the Empire" that is, the United Kingdom and her self-governing Dominions, with a view to work together in

(2) "developing and helping forward the governed" which means India, Egypt, and the Crown Colonies. And, in the performance of this task, "a positive policy of development by preferences, by bounties, by steamship subsidies, by the vigorous building of railways, by well-equipped agricultural and forestry and mining department, must be carried out."

VI

THE WAR AND THE OLD IMPERIALISM

THE bitter experiences of the last world-war which are said to have revolutionised the life and outlook of the British nation in so many directions have not evidently affected by the *Times* ten years ago. We in India did at one time think that these experiences would bring home to British statesmanship the wisdom and urgency of adopting a policy of trust in regard both to India and Egypt, which would remove the badge of political serfdom from these two ancient countries, and place them upon a footing of equality with the self-governing members of the Empire, and thus secure their permanent allegiance to the Imperial connection. But the dramatic ending of the war has practically left the British the masters of the present world-situation for the time being, has practically dissipated this idea.

Great hopes were aroused in our educated countrymen by the call for Imperial Reconstruction sounded all over the Empire during the early months of the War. The war-situation forced this problem upon responsible statesmen both in Great Britain and the Dominions. British statesmen felt the unfairness of asking the Dominions to make such huge sacrifices both in men and money for the defence of an Empire, in the determination of whose Imperial policy they had really no voice. Mr. Lloyd George openly said so. It was to conciliate Colonial sentiments in regard to this matter that he sent out an invitation to Colonial premiers and other representatives of the Colonial governments to come and join the Imperial War Cabinet to jointly deliberate upon the vital question of "how to win the war." Mr. Lloyd George's Cabinet thus expanded itself, without any change in the law and constitution of the United Kingdom, into practically a Council of the Empire. It was undoubtedly a very clever stroke of statesmanship of a sort. It gave to the Empire a symbol and instrument of its collective life and interests—and, even to some extent, of its collective authority, without any formal discussion of it by any council or conference of the representatives of the Imperial family, that might raise inconvenient questions regarding the number and authority of the representation that would have to be given to the different Dominions. The Cabinet in Westminister continued, in theory, the sole and supreme custodian of Imperial interests and Imperial authority. The British Premier invited the Dominions representatives to join his Cabinet, in what may be called its

Imperial side, just as he invited his colleagues in the British Parliament to join it in its national side; and, in both cases he secured the formal assent of his King. He did not create any well-defined constitutional right, but only established a *precedent* which might, should the course of Imperial history and evolution demand it, gradually become a right. By this clever stroke Mr. Lloyd George removed the urgency of the problem of constitutional reconstruction of the Empire, that had loomed so large during the earlier months of the war.

As regards India, the recognition given to it "as an important part of the British Commonwealth" and its representation on the Imperial Cabinet through nominees of the Government of India will mean, in plain English, that Great Britain will have these additional seats on it, as the Power specially responsible for the peace, order and good government of this Dependency and the happiness and well-being of its voiceless populations. The recognition given to India by the Imperial War Conference of 1917, with the consent of the two "Indian representatives" present there, as "an important part" of the Empire, really means the recognition only of her status *as a Dependency;* with this difference that, while she was hitherto a Dependency of Great Britain only, henceforth she will be recognised as a Dependency of the whole of the self-governing section of the Empire. The Imperial Conference of 1917, thus, puts its seal and authority upon the policy adumbrated nine years before by the *Times,* and practically identified itself with the Imperialism of the *Times*-Milner school!

In fact, the character of British Imperialism has not changed during the last ten years. Lord Milner still inspires Imperial policy from his place in the Imperial Cabinet. In the midst of the war, in the summer of 1916, addressing the representatives of the Dominion Parliaments then on a visit to England, Lord Milner said:—

> "It would needlessly complicate the task immediately before us, which is that of devising means by which the Dominions can share with the United Kingdom in the supreme control of the Empire—if we were to try and deal at the same time with the future of India, where self-government is in its infancy or with that of the other Dependencies, in which it exists in various degrees or does not exist at all. To say that is not to deny that a day may come when having proved themselves capable of local autonomy, some or all of them will be entitled to representation in the Imperial Parliament. But the time at which and the extent to which such representation should be accorded to

> them are quite unforseeable at present, and to give it them, while local self-government is still in its rudimentary stages, would be putting the cart before the horse."

In the same year, about the same time, a series of articles appeared in the *Times*, seeking to discuss the problem of after-war Imperial Reconstruction, which practically followed the lines adopted by the *Times* in 1909.

VII

PROGRAMME OF AFTER-WAR RECONSTRUCTION

THESE articles have since been reprinted and published in book form, with the title —"Elements of Reconstruction"; and it is significant that Lord Milner has been induced to lend his authority to these by writing an introduction to this small book. Coming to discuss "the dream of a Council of the whole Empire, the dream of defining by some comprehensive constitutional law, the at-present-extraordinarily-informal relations of the various parts of the Empire" —the writers say :—

> "Every body perceives that the Government of Britain is not really representative of the Empire it rules; Great Britain is remarkably in the position

of a trustee minding the affairs of various kindred minors and of various races and communities temporarily incapacitated from independent sovereignty, and almost every body feels this must necessarily be a temporary arrangement and that what is desirable marches with what is just, when we look to a recasting of this complicated system of relationships in which Great Britain will no longer be sole director but merely a partner in partnership with its former dependencies. So far as the Dominions go, that are predominantly of British descent, the Dominions that are pleased to be called Britains beyond the seas, it is quite conceivable that there may be political unifications of a very thorough sort, but so far as the great masses of non-British people go, people with alien racial and national traditions, the idea of assimilation is equally unacceptable with the idea of continuing and unending subjection. Ireland has taught the British the folly of rash and premature experiments in amalgamation, and it is clear that the future of the non-kindred parts of the Empire, such as Egypt or Rajputana or Bengal, lies along the line of education and autonomous development to the position of free and equal allies in one great Imperial Confederation. So far as these non-British peoples are concerned, it may be questioned whether the setting up of any common Imperial Council to include them is advisable. So far as they are concerned it may be wiser at present for the trustee to continue to administer."

"That does not mean an arrest of political development. It means that these mainly Oriental dependencies, which are now in phases of profound economic reconstruction and which are emerging rather rapidly from ancient and primitive political conditions to the possession of a Press, and to a steadily increasing racial and national self-consciousness, have still to show their quality and difference under modern conditions, have still to shape. They may presently be plainly developing on lines so similar to the lines in the development of our own community that our sons may be able to take up the question of an equal and parallel share in common Empire with some confidence ; or they may display so essential and incurable a divergence that the problem may have become manifestly the problem of an alliance of dissimilars. We know too little to foretell which of these directions will be taken, and meanwhile we submit that the general policy of the Imperial Government is to keep things going, to release every tendency that does not threaten the safety of the Empire, to give the native every chance and every opportunity that is not plainly mischievous, to encourage experiment as much as possible and to direct it as little as possible, and in and out of season, steadily, persistently, to set up and maintain in the minds of ruling race and subject race alike this idea of the trustee, the idea of "when you are ready to take it back, your land is yours." Upon which lines of thought it is clear that the idea of a council representative of the Empire recedes also from our problem."

VIII

THE "TRUSTEE" IDEA

THE idea so frankly presented here stands clearly at the back of the Montagu-Chelmsford Scheme of constitutional reforms in India. It is present, indeed, in the very terms of the Announcement of August 20, 1917, in pursuance of which these Reforms have been formulated. This Announcement, while accepting the progressive realisation of responsible government in India as an integral part of the British Empire, as the goal of British policy, claims that "the British Government and the Government of India on whom the responsibility lies for the welfare and advancement of the Indian peoples must be the judges of the time and measure of each advance and they must be guided by the co-operation received from those upon whom new opportunities of service will be conferred, and by the extent to which it is found that confidence can be reposed in their sense of responsibility."

This trustee-idea supplies both the rational and the moral justification of this claim. The authors of the new reform proposals have based their scheme upon this idea. This is proved by the following quotation from a hundred and twenty years old utterance of Sir Thomas Munro with which they have topped their discussion of the problem of Indian reform.

> "What is to be final results of our arrangements on the character of the people? Is it to be raised, is it to be lowered? Are we to be satisfied with merely securing our power and protecting the inhabitants or are we to endeavour to raise their character, to

render them worthy of filling higher stations in the management of their country and devising plans for its improvement? We should look on India not as a temporary possession, but as one to be maintained permanently until the natives shall in some future age have abandoned most of their superstitions and prejudices and become sufficiently enlightened to frame a regular government for themselves and to conduct and preserve it.

The fact that the authors of the Report on Indian Constitutional Reforms have accepted this statement of Sir Thomas Munro, both as a justification and a defence of their scheme, conclusively proves the complete identity of this "New Policy" with that adumbrated ten years ago in the Empire Day Supplement of the *Times* and which has been more recently re-stated in the "Elements of Reconstruction." This trustee-idea runs indeed through every argument and proposal of the Montagu-Chelmsford Report.

It is time, however, that this pretentious plea was thoroughly exposed in the interest as much of India as of the Empire. Without questioning the honesty of it, it must be pointed out that this trustee-idea is as false in theory as it is inevitably hurtful to Indian interests in practice; while by obscuring vital issues and obstructing timely reconciliation between Indian and Imperial interests, it offers a very serious menace to the peaceful perpetuation of India's connection with the Empire.

This plea served some useful purpose in the earlier stages of our British connection when the tendency of the administration of the British East India Company was to encourage unrestrained exploitation of the country and its people by British traders in India who ran the new Government specially for their own personal aggrandisement and the profit of their employers in their homeland. Without stopping this exploitation, the trustee-idea did in those days seek to apply a moral brake to the process. As long as no one except the holders of the East India stocks was directly interested in Indian exploitation, this idea lent moral motive to disinterested British politicians to protect the people of India from the maladministration of the East India Company. Gradually, however, with the birth of British industrialism, following upon the discovery of steam power and the invention of machineries, an increasing body of political and economic interests was created in England in the administration and exploitation of India. Since then administration and exploitation have gone hand in hand in the government of this great Dependency. With the growth of this new condition, the old moral value of this plea has been entirely destroyed, though the old habit of using it not as of old, for the protection of Indian interests, but for the indefinite prolongation of India's political and economic "minority," has persisted even to this day.

But, even those who claim that its compensations have been both ample and solid in the case of India, cannot possibly deny the truth of the general proposition that the political domination by one people over another creates inevitable conflicts of interests between the ruling and the subject race. This conflict is present even in national governments which are controlled by a ruling class, whether, they are the king and the aristocracy of the land, or the upper middle classes, the *bourgoise* as they are called in France. This conflict of interests is infinitely more keen and extensive in the autocratic rule of one race or nation over another weaker or less organised race or nation, than it is in class-rule, or even in the government of the people by individual despots supported by a section, representing either the power of wealth or the authority of religion among them.

IX

THE "TRUSTEE" WITH "ADVERSE INTERESTS"

BUT, every apologist of British rule in India has, for the last one hundred and fifty years, persistently ignored this fact, and sought to justify this apparent political injustice, to their own enlightened conscience by the fancy of this trust-idea, forgetting the obvious truth that no law or court of justice in civilisation permits or tolerates the appointment of any person to the charge of a minor's estate who has obviously adverse interests in that estate. For, it cannot be denied that British and Indian interests have never been identical in the government of this country. The *Times* frankly admits it, though possibly without an adequate sense of the meaning and significance of this admission, in the various pleas which it has put forward in support of its Imperialist ideal. "The administration of the Dependent Empire," we are told, "not only provides a career for thousands of Englishmen to-day, but creates a class of men whose official experience and high standard of public duty are undoubtedly an addition to our (*i.e.*, British) national life." It ignores, however, what this means to the "national life" of the Dependent Empire. Every provision in the administration of India for the employment of Englishmen to posts carrying high salary and great responsibility, means so much economic, intellectual, and moral loss to the people. What is England's gain is India's loss. Whatever compensations we may have had for it, in other directions, this fact cannot be gainsaid. And it proves "adverse" interest in those who claim to be our "trustees."

This "adverse" interest is much larger in the economic and industrial field. Whatever plea of our political or administrative incapacity may be put forward, in justification of the administrative domination of the British people over us, no one can say or suggest that Indian arts and crafts had no place in the markets of the world, when the British first came to this country. And, who has killed all these? Let an English historian, Horace Hayman Wilson, answer this question:—

> "It is also a melancholy instance of the wrong done to India by the country on which she has become dependent. It was stated in evidence in 1813, that the cotton and silk goods of India, up to the period, could be sold for a profit in the British market at a price from 50 to 60 per cent. lower than those fabricated in England. It consequently became necessary to protect the latter

by duties of 70 to 80 per cent. on their value or by positive prohibition. Had this not been the case, had not such prohibitory duties and decrees existed, the mills of Paisley and Manchester would have been stopped in their outset, and could scarcely have again been set in motion even by the power of steam. They were created by the sacrifice of the Indian manufacture. Had India been independent, she would have retaliated, would have imposed prohibitory duties upon British goods, and would thus have preserved her productive industry from annihilation. This act of self-defence was not permitted her; she was at the mercy of the stranger. British goods were forced upon her without paying any duty, and the foreign manufacturer employed the arm of political injustice to keep down and ultimately strangle a competitor with whom he could not have contended on equal terms."

The facts quoted by Wilson are old; but the adverse British interests in the economic and industrial life of India, which they prove, still exist. And their presence completely establishes the unfairness of the plea of trustee-ship upon which Great Britain still seeks to satisfy her conscience and the civilised world in regard to her enjoyment of autocratic authority in the government of India.

This trust-idea, so frequently put forward by the supporters of the present political authority in India, is logically untrue, morally unjustifiable, and practically impossible, owing first, to the presence of undeniable and inevitable conflicts of interests between the trustee and his charge; and secondly, to the absence of any Power or Authority which, standing over both the trustee and the trust, might remedy any wrong which the former might be tempted to do to the latter. It is quite time that all parties frankly recognised this fact. Because this recognition is essential to the discovery and application of some rational and just principle of reconciliation between legitimate British and undoubted Indian interests in the political and economic administration of this country,—a reconciliation that alone can be expected to safeguard and perpetuate India's Imperial connection upon which hangs the future of both India and the Empire.

If, indeed, we had any Supreme Court of Justice to adjudicate between the trustee and his trust, in India's political and economic relations with England, and if Great Britain were called upon to render an honest account of the management of the trust, such as is required by every British court of every trustee in private life, she would find the task absolutely hopeless.

Every trustee is, of course, justly entitled to compensate himself for the time and labour he is called upon to spend in the management of the trust. In this view, the Government at Westminister would be legitimately entitled to levy a definite tribute, year after year, for the government of India. The British Government would also have every right to employ whomsoever it thought competent for the practical administration of the affairs of its charge and pay them out of the assets of the trust such remuneration or reward as might be deemed necessary for such services. These remunerations and rewards might even be unreasonably extravagant. The men so employed might even be aliens. And their pay and pensions, spent largely outside India, might involve some economic loss to the country, such as the employment of indigenous agencies might prevent. But these could be charitably attributed to the exigencies of the situation, and at most to mere recklessness, and therefore, could be overlooked or even condoned, out of regard for the larger compensations of an "enlightened rule."

But Great Britain did a lot more, which could, under no conceivable circumstance, be reasonably justified by the trust-idea.

X

WHAT THE TRUSTEE HAS NOT DONE

FOR the last 150 years the economic resources of our country have been increasingly exploited by foreign, particularly British, capitalists, working under the protecting wing of the British authority in India. It cannot be denied that this foreign exploitation has developed these resources to a considerable extent. But the profits of these new developments have not come to the people nor contributed to strengthen the economic staying-power of the nation.

We have earned only the wages of our labour; and these wages also have gone back, to a very large extent, to these foreign exploiters themselves, in the shape of the price for imported commodities that have been thrust upon us, leaving practically little or no margin of these increased wages either to the wage-earner himself or to his people.

The generalisations deduced from the experience of European countries in this matter are, therefore, absolutely inapplicable to Indian conditions. Increased wages in Great Britain or Germany or America mean greater comfort and higher standards of living for the masses. The wages which a labourer earns there is distributed among his own people and remains in the country, increasing the wealth of the nation. Thirty years ago no American or British workman could live in a decent house or enjoy the luxury of an organ or a piano. Few of them could provide themselves with cut flowers for their table, or pots for their windows or carpets for their sitting rooms. All these are found now in the houses of many working men in America and the United Kingdom. Many of them are able to-day to provide themselves with lovely bicycles. These are undoubted evidences of the increasing wealth and prosperity of their country. The price of the organ or the harmonium which the British or American working-man pays out of his own increased earnings goes to the manufacturer of these in his own country; the value of the flowers and pots goes to British and American gardeners, that of the bicycles to the British or American manufacturers, and of the carpets to those who make them in their own country. Very little of the increased wages which the working-man earns to-day is spent upon imported luxuries and is, thereby, really lost to the country.

But all this is very different in India. The copy-book economists who cite the high standard of living of the present-day agriculturists and labouring classes in

India, as evidence of our material progress, do not stop to consider how much of the things that contribute to this so-called higher standard are manufactured in the country, and how much of these come from abroad. The shirts and coats, unknown to their forefathers, which are seen on the person of our poorer classes to-day are made of imported stuff, and the value of these articles, less the wages of the local tailors and the profit of the middleman who trade in these stuffs, goes to foreign manufacturers and alien merchants engaged in our import trade. The same remark applies to those who rush to the conclusion that the increased use of shoes and umbrellas by our rural populations are a proof of the advancing economic progress and prosperity of the country. And the moment we probe these things deeply, we discover that all the modern developments of our resources, worked with the help of foreign capital and the agencies of foreign capitalists and traders, have not really contributed to our economic advancement or to the increased economic staying-power of our people. This is the simple and obvious solution of the enigma of the increasing poverty of a country, the material resources of which have enormously increased during the last hundred years. This material advancement has only helped to increase our economic dependence and has made the way clear for the perpetuation of our economic serfdom.

The absence of fluid capital and industrial enterprise in the country stood, and still stands, in the way of the adequate development of our immense natural resources, it is true. Foreign capital was, and is even to-day, very largely needed for the development of India's material resources. This need cannot, and indeed, need not be denied or ignored. But the question is,—how would a national government meet this essential necessity? Would it invite foreign capitalists to come and freely exploit the economic possibilities of the country? Or, would it not simply float the necessary loans in foreign money-markets, on the guarantee of the national credit, and, if necessary, even by giving a lien on certain heads of national revenue to the subscribers of these foreign loans, and thus secure to the country the *entire* profits of these new "developments", less such proportion of these as might have to be paid as interest and reserved as sinking fund for the re-payment of these loans? By this means the borrowed capital would, after a term of years, be an addition to national capital, employed in fresh developments of the nation's undeveloped resources. The Government of India did follow this method, to some extent, in the construction of what are known as reproductive public works. The construction of what are known as "guaranteed railways" also partly followed this policy; though consideration for the foreign holders of these railway-bonds has, in some cases, deferred the complete assumption of state-ownership over some of these railways, including the most profitable ones, even after the term of the lease was over. But, though this latter act may, perhaps, be counted as a violation of the "trust", so far as the general policy of undertaking reproductive public works with capital borrowed from foreign countries goes, it is what even a national government would do, and is, therefore, fully consistent with perfect loyalty to the trust.

The British Government in India could have adopted a similar policy in regard to our general economic development also. It could have easily offered the credit of the State in India, if need be, guaranteed by the

Government of the United Kingdom, as trustee of the Indian people, to indigenous concerns and thus helped them to put their debentures with the interest due on them guaranteed by it, upon the British markets, and thereby induce British and other foreign capital to come to this country; and, though part of the profits of these enterprises might go out of the country, the working expenses would come to the pockets of the people and be spent entirely in the country; and what is far more important, the training and experience which the management of these businesses would give to the people would be an intellectual and moral asset to the nation of almost incalculable value, which would encourage indigenous capital to have confidence in national business enterprises, and thus gradually help the people to attain economic freedom and self-sufficiency. This policy was practically followed by Japan in working out her industrial regeneration. If a similar policy was not adopted in India, it was due, mainly, to want either of foresight or of loyalty to their trust, of our so-called trustee-government. If the Government of India were absolutely faithful to their trust, they would have protected our ancient manufactures and helped the new ones by a system of protective tariffs, which might even be retaliatory, as Wilson points out, in the case of British imports.

And, above all else, a national government, even if it did encourage the flow of foreign capital for the development of the agricultural and mineral resources of the country, would strictly preserve the sovereign rights of the people to their own land, and to everything it held in its womb, by an absolute prohibition of the acquisition of any right on these by any foreigner. Even where private ownership of land was recognised or conceded, the right of transferring this to foreigners might well and legitimately be taken away from these private owners by positive legislation. Even if temporary leases were permitted to be granted to foreigners, the conditions of such lease might have been determined by law, with a view to prevent hurtful exploitation by foreign capitalists and adventurers. Lastly, where foreign capitalists employed Indian labour upon any large scale, a national government would certainly safeguard national interests by special fiscal and factory legislation, specially devised to preserve to the labourer and to the State, a reasonable share of the profits of these enterprises, and to provide adequately for the physical health and intellectual education of the labour-populations. A trustee in private life is required to administer the estate of the trust exactly in the same way, with the same regard for the interests of his charge, as the latter might be expected reasonably to do himself. When one nation assumes the government of another nation, really, as a "trust", it is expected to administer the affairs of the latter exactly with the same care and consideration for its interests, as the subject nation, if they had a national government, might be reasonably expected to do under present conditions. Loyalty to the "turst" and a concern for the duties and responsibilities which it imposed upon the trustee would have led the Government of India to pursue the line of policy which a national government would pursue, for the protection of national interests, the promotion of national efficiency, and the advancement of national credit. Have the British Government done this? Let history answer.

XI

"ADMINISTRATION" AND "EXPLOITATION"

NOR can it be seriously urged that this failure is entirely or even largely due to the ignorance or incapacity of the "trustee", and that the Government of India wanted, but could not follow, owing to insuperable practical difficulties and circumstances beyond their control, a policy more consistent with the moral obligations which their position as "trustee" imposed upon them. In fact, though individual British politicians and statesmen have occasionally realised these obligations, the political conscience of the "trustee"-nation has rarely or never sufficiently quickened with this sense, to initiate or control Indian policy. On the other hand, the process of foreign exploitation, thoughtlessly and unconsciously encouraged in the earlier years of our British connection, by the British rulers of India, has gradually developed into a conscious aim, and has become part of an organised policy of British Imperialism.

For a very long time past a systematic attempt has, in fact, been made to deliberately ignore the evils which this foreign exploitation has brought about. Lord Curzon went so far indeed as to publicly defend this exploitation, and declared that, when rightly viewed, "exploitation and administration were parts of the same duty in the government of India". His lordship made this statement to a company of British miners at Jheria, completely ignoring the fact that of all kinds of foreign exploitation that of the mining resources of a country is the most hurtful, because the minerals, once taken out are taken out for good; and when the profits of these go through foreign pockets to foreign countries, it inflicts a loss upon the people which can never be recouped or even compensated, indirectly, by any other advantage which the exploration of the mines may bring. Addressing the tea-planters of Silchar, Lord Curzon declared :—

> "I look upon all Englishmen in this country (and if any Scotchmen or Irishmen are present, pray do not let them think that I am excluding them) as engaged in different branches of the same great undertaking. Here we are all fellow-countrymen, comrades, and friends. The fact that some of us earn our livelihood or discharge our duty by the work of administration, and others by cultivating the soil, does not differentiate us one from the other. These are merely the sub-divisions of labour. They are not distinctions of object, or purpose, or aim."

Lord Curzon had little patience with those who were constantly "talking copy-book fallacies about the economic drain", and said, in one of his parting speeches in India:—

> When I hear the employment of British capital in India deplored, I feel tempted to ask where, without it, would have been Calcutta? Where would have been Bombay? Where would have been our railways, our shipping, our river navigation, our immense and prosperous trade? And, why should a different argument be applied to India from any other country in the world? When Great Britain poured her wealth into South America and China, I have never heard those countries complain that they were being ruined. No one pities Egypt when a foreign nation resuscitates her industries and dams the Nile. It was foreign capital and foreign brains

that exploited the industries of Russia, which are now beginning to be a source of such profit to that country. When America floods England, as she is doing, with the resources of her accumulated capital, her amazing inventiveness, and her commercial genius, none of us at home sits down and bewails our cruel lot at being bled by a foreign drain. I therefore would say to the people of this country—if my words would have the slightest effect —look facts in the face. Recognise that capital does not wrap itself in the flag of any one country. It is international. It is like the wind which bloweth where it listeth, and comes and goes as it will. The whole industrial and mercantile world is one great field for the tiller to till: and if the man who lives on the spot will not cultivate it with his own spade, then he has no

> right to blame the outsider who enters it with his plough."

It is needless to expose the obvious fallacy of Lord Curzon's plea. Capital, in our time, is no doubt "international"; "and the whole industrial and mercantile world is one great field for the tiller to till," but it cannot pursue its own object without regard to the supreme economic, industrial, and even political interests of the different peoples among whom history had parcelled out this "great field." British capital cannot work in South America or Russia or even in China, in the same way as it has and is doing in India. If Lord Curzon's theory of the international character of capital be correct, one may ask, why should not German capital be admitted, even if it may not be invited, into Great Britain or the British Dominions, or into India, upon the same terms and with the same measure of freedom, as British capital is employed or admitted? However might this "poser" have been answered before the war, the declared policy of the United Kingdom to-day is to prevent the exploitation of any part of the British Empire, in any shape or form, by German capital or German enterprise, and the Imperial Cabinet has been devising quite a variety of means to protect the economic and industrial interests of the Empire, both severally and collectively, against hurtful competition from Germany and other "enemy" countries.

XII

FOREIGN CAPITAL AND NATIONAL AUTONOMY

IN fact, this trustee-idea, which the *Times* wants both the governing and the Depending Empire to constantly bear in mind, during the period of education and transition through which the latter must pass before it can be safely admitted to partnership with the self-governing dominions, has not only not helped to protect the vital economic interests of the "trust," but has, on the contrary, always found an excuse to oppose the progress of political freedom and national autonomy in India, for fear lest it should be hurtful to foreign capitalist interests in the country. Convincing proof of this is found even in the Montagu-

Chelmsford Report which proposed to initiate the first steps towards responsible government in pursuance of the Announcement of August 20, 1917. The Montagu-Chelmsford proposals started with the initial reservation that whatever reforms may be undertaken, and whatever rights may be conferred on the people of India, the autocratic powers of the Governor-General in Council, which is called the "Government of India" in these proposals, must be absolutely maintained, subject, of course, to such limitations as the responsibility of this Government to the British Cabinet and the British Parliament may impose. In Para 190 of the Report, the following formula has been laid down :—

> "The Government of India must remain wholly responsible to Parliament, and owing such responsibility, its authority in essential matters must remain indisputable, pending experience of the

effect of the changes now to be introduced in the provinces."

In Para 266 of the Report this principle is re-affirmed:—"We have already made our opinion clear that pending the development of responsible government in the provinces, the Government of India must remain responsible only to Parliament. In other words, *in all matters which it judges to be essential to the discharge of its responsibilities for peace, order, and good government, it must, saving only its responsibility to Parliament, retain indisputable power.*"

What the nature of Parliamentary control over the Government of India has been we all know. Parliament not only "may sometimes be," as the M-C. Report says, but has almost invariably been "a sleepy guardian of Indian interests." The Government of India no doubt requires that the Governor-General in Council shall "pay due obedience to all such orders" as he may receive from the Secretary of State; but it is evident that the nature of this control "must vary with the interest shown by Parliament on whose behalf the Secretary of State exercises these powers." And the M-C. Report frankly admits that:—

"If resentment has been felt in India that there has been a tendency on occasions to treat Viceroys of India as "agents" of the British Government, it is fair to add that *there have been periods when Viceroys have almost regarded Secretaries of State as the convenient mouthpiece of their policy in Parliament. Certainly there have been times when the power of the Government of India rested actually far less upon the support of the Cabinet and Parliament than on the respect which its reputation for efficiency inspired. The hands of the Government of India were strong:*

and there was little disposition to question the quality of their work, so long as it was concerned chiefly with material things, and the subtler springs of action which lie in the mental development of a people were not aroused."

The Italics are mine, and these admissions prove the almost illusory character of the responsibility of the Government of India to the British Cabinet and the British Parliament. In another place, Para 268, the illustrious authors of the Report on Constitutional Reforms, admit that they know—"how rarely Parliament asserts its powers, how little interest and time it devotes to Indian affairs." Indeed, they fully justify this absence of effective Parliamentary control over the Government of India; because "constant interference by Parliament in the affairs of a distant Asiatic country would have greatly increased the difficulties of its administration." The practical result of this absence of practical Parliamentary control of the Indian administration has been to make the Government of India practically irresponsible. In matters where Parliament does not affect it, the duty or responsibility of the Government of India is to "its own conscience"—or, perhaps, as the authors of the M-C. Report put it, "to its successors in office" only, and to no one else. And all these things must be borne in mind, while judging the fundamental reservation which the M-C. scheme made in favour of the autocratic authority and powers of the Government of India. Recommendation No. 5 in the Summary in Appendix I of the Report said:

"The Government of India to preserve indisputable authority on matters adjudged by it to be essential in the discharge of its responsibility for peace, order, and good government."

In No. 15 of this Summary of Recommendations, the term "good government" is made to include "sound financial administration." The phrase—"sound financial administration"—is left, however, without any definition or explanation.

How this undefined, and we are afraid, practically undefinable phrase, "sound financial administration" may be conveniently interpreted, may be gathered from Chapter XI of the Report, and particularly from Sub-sections (iii) and (iv) of it, which deal with "Industries and tariffs" and "The Non-official Community" respectively. This Non-official Community mean (i) the European Commercial Community, whose position is considered in Para 344; (ii) Foreign Christian Missions, discussed in Para 345; and (iii) The Anglo-Indian or Eurasian Community, who are the subject of Para 346. Of these, Para 344 is the most important, as indicating the true inwardness of the extreme caution with which the M-C. scheme was prepared, and the real aim and intention of the checks and counter-checks, which it provided; and, it may well be quoted here in full:—

"We cannot conclude without taking into due account the presence of a considerable community of non-official Europeans in India. In the main, they are engaged in commercial enterprises, but, besides those, are the missions, European and American, which in furthering education, building up character and inculcating healthier domestic habits have done work for which India should be grateful. There are also an appreciable number of retired officials and others whose working life has been given to India, settled in the cooler parts of the country. When complaints are rife that European commercial interests are selfish and drain the country of wealth which it ought to retain, it is well to remind ourselves how much of India's material prosperity is due to European commerce. It is true that those engaged in commerce mix less than officials with educated Indians, and that may be a reason why the latter do not always recognise their claim on India's consideration. Like commercial people all the world over Englishmen in business in India are frankly uninterested in politics; many of them would readily admit that they have taken insufficient part both in municipal business and the business of government. Our concern, however, is not so much with the past as with the future. From discussions with them we know that many of them accept the trends of events, and are fully prepared to see Indian political development proceed. India has benefited enormously by her commercial development in European hands; nor is the benefit less because it was incidental and not the purpose of the undertaking. What then are the obligations of the various parties? Clearly it is the duty of British commerce in India to identify itself with the interests of India, which are higher than the interests of any community; to take part in political life; to use its considerable wealth and opportunities to commend itself to India; and having demonstrated both its value and its good intentions, to content to rest like other industries on the new foundation of government in the wishes of the people. No less is it the duty of Indian politicians to respect the expectations which have been implicitly held out; to remember how India has profited by commercial development which only British capital and enterprise achieved; to bethink themselves that though the capital invested in private enterprises was not borrowed under any assurances that the existing form of government would endure, yet the favourable terms on which money was obtained for India's development were undoubtedly affected by the fact of British rule; and to abstain from advocating differential treatment aimed not so much at promoting Indian as at injuring British commerce. Finally, it is our duty to reserve to the Government the power to protect any industry from prejudicial attack or privileged competition. This obligation is imposed upon it, if not by history, at least by the duty of protecting capital, credit and indeed property without discrimination."—Para 344, M-C. Report.

And, as these assurances had not removed the apprehensions of the European commercial community in India, the Viceroy (Lord Chelmsford) took pains in his opening speech of the winter session of the Imperial Legislative Council at Delhi on February 6, 1919, to "emphasise their intentions" in regard to this phase of the proposed constitutional reforms in India.

> "Let me turn to the very important matter of British commercial interests in this country. It would distress me profoundly if I thought that we could with justice be accused of under-rating either the colossal financial interests at stake or the enormous part which British non-official energy, character and brains have played in the task of making India what she is. For myself, I regarded these facts as self-evident, and thought it was not necessary to re-assure this important community. We had in our Report made

our attitude towards them quite clear. However, the complaint has been made that we have dealt too summarily with the subject. So let me emphasise our intentions. I have not found, by the way, in the papers of a year ago, or the criticism just received, any reasoned statement of the ways in which it is supposed that the British trade-interest may be jeopardised by the changes which we have in view. I note, however, that in the joint-address, which some representatives of the European commerce in Calcutta signed last year, reference was made to the risk of injury by "predatory or regulative legislation" or the neglect of transportation and other facilities; and I see that the Bengal Chamber of Commerce appear to have chiefly in mind the proposals for provincial taxation likely to prejudice commerce or industry.

Now, let me explain the position, as I see it. The legislation, on which British commerce in the main depends, is mainly All-India in character. Some of it is embodied in the great commercial codes; some of it deals with matters of factories, petroleum, explosives or mines. Now, in as much as these will remain with the Government of India, which will, as I have laid down more than once, retain indisputable authority, there is surely no reasonable ground for apprehension. Commerce can make its voice heard just as effectively as heretofore. It may be said, however, that in the future Provincial Councils will exercise more freely the power of amending the All-India Acts. But, that they can only do with the previous sanction of the Governor-General. In any case, there is the safeguard of the triple veto of the Governor, the Governor-General and the Crown, and this applies to all provincial legislation. It seems to me, indeed, that the control of the matters of peculiar interest to European commerce is, to a great extent, concentrated in the hands of the Government of India. I am thinking of the tariff and the currency, of banking, railways, shipping, posts and telegraphs. In these respects no existing measure of security is being diminished and therefore the apprehension is surely groundless. But evidently it is in the minds of some people that in the provincial sphere it will be possible injuriously to affect the commercial community say, for instance, by special interests being singled out to bear the burden of provincial taxation, or by rival interests being artificially stimulated. What protection will there be in such cases? Well, the Secretary of State and I have pledged ourselves in paragraph 344 to reserve to the Government power to protect any industry from prejudiced attack or privileged competition. To speak for myself, I believe this can be secured by embodying this undertaking in the instrument of instructions given to the Governor on appointment, wherein he will be informed that His Majesty's Government lay on him a responsibility for seeing that the pledge is made good. With such a public document in his hands the Governor, with the Government of India and the Secretary of State behind him, would be in a very strong position to resist all proposals of his Ministers which appeared to be acts of hostility to British commerce. There will, moreover, be representatives of that interest sitting in the Provincial Chamber, and

> I cannot do them the injustice of supposing that they will fail to bring any just grievance effectively to the Governor's notice, or, if need be, to remind him of his responsibility."

Nobody refuses to admit that under the peculiar conditions of India foreign capital was, and is still, wanted for the development of our resources and the evolution of our economic life along, what may be called, modern lines. The circumstances in which the British East India Company found us when it first came to trade with us soon commenced to change. It was no longer possible for India to keep pace with modern industrial and economic evolution in the wide world about her with her old and simple systems of trade and credit and her ancient appliances of production.

But what the Indian economists and politicians contend is that they should have been encouraged and helped to advance along their own national lines, consistently with the preservation of their special social and economic structure and the character of their special culture and civilisation. The processes of economic exploitation started by the nation which had acquired political authority over them, however, ignored the past of their subjects, refused practically their claims to any high civilisation or social evolution, and sought to force upon them their own ideals and impose upon their primitive moulds the heavy frame-work of an alien economic and industrial society. And herein lay the grave evils of the so-called economic "development" which has been worked in India with the help of British capital and the agency of British capitalists and adventurers. And the greatest tragedy of it all is that the Government of India has never had any appreciation of these fatal consequences. And the result has been that the process of this fatal foreign exploitation thoughtlessly encouraged in the earlier years of our British connection has gradually developed into a conscious aim and has become now a part of the settled and organised policy of British Imperialism.

XIII

DOMINANT BRITISH ECONOMIC THOUGHT

THE last war, which has worked many changes in the life and outlook of the British people and their rulers, has not only worked no change in this economic ideal of British Imperialism; but, on the contrary, has lent fresh inspiration to it. After-War Economic Reconstruction, of which we heard a good deal during the progress of the war, and specially in the earlier years of it, obviously means better and more effective methods of this Imperialist exploitation. This is the real meaning and intention of the abandonment of free Trade and the adoption of what is called Imperial preference, an admittedly aggressive policy of Protection, by the British Cabinet.

But this new departure in British economic policy means, indeed, a good deal more than what the term Imperial Preference connotes on the face of it. It is really the beginning of a far-reaching economic revolution in British policy and Imperial development. Economic Protection ordinarily means the protection of home industries from hurtful foreign competitions by the imposition of preventive or prohibitive tariffs upon foreign imports competing with home products in home markets. This protection is a sound economic policy only when it protects infant or nascent national industries which have reasonable prospects of attaining a healthy and vigorous state if they are not killed by unfair competition of fully-developed foreign industries. After a national industry has attained what may be called full maturity, there can be no justification for the maintenance of any protective tariffs. Viewed from this standpoint, economic protection means only a measure of national insurance for the benefit of growing and hopeful national industries. One generation pays more for the articles it uses and which enjoy this protection, so that another generation may pay less, even under a state of normal free-trade. Wherever protection is adopted with this object, it is fully justified. But at best it must always be a temporary device, just like the railings with which valuable saplings are protected from harm from animals that love to make their meals out of them. When the sapling grows up into its proper stature and strength and is protected by its own trunk and bark from the depradations of its enemies, there is no need for keeping up the artificial protections. Even so must be the case with infant and weak industries.

In this view, India needed protection for her nascent or latent economic or industrial possibilities. This protection she needed mainly against Great Britain herself. But no Cabinet at Westminister dared give her this much-needed protection for fear of losing the Lancashire vote, which was the greatest stronghold of British Liberalism for so many decades past. On the contrary, even when an import duty on cotton had to be imposed for purely revenue purposes, it had to be abandoned under pressure from Lancashire. When India began to start cotton mills and the produce of these mills commenced to threaten the Eastern Asiatic trade of Lancashire mill-owners, they brought all their political influence to bear upon the Government in London and through them upon the Government of India to impose an excise duty on Indian cotton yarns and cotton goods of certain counts in regard to which there had grown up a competition between Bombay and Manchester. All these are familiar facts which go to show how Indian economic interests have been systematically sacrificed to satisfy British capitalist interests.

There is absolutely no reason to hope that all this will change in the near future. On the contrary, the new economic policy which is being insidiously advanced by the dominant school of present-day British Imperialism offers a very serious menace to India's economic freedom and future. This policy, as we have seen, had been foreshadowed ten years back in the remarkable pronouncement of the *Times* which has been noticed in a previous chapter. But while the *Times* pleaded for protective tariffs and steamship and other subsidies for helping private capitalist enterprise to exploit the immense natural resources of the dependent Empire, which is also the tropical Empire, and for the maintenance and advancement of the industries of the self-governing Empire which is almost wholly situate in the temperate zone. The latest development of this economic policy of the Empire has called for the more radical policy of direct and open participation of the State in the material exploitation of the resources of the dependent Empire. And herein lies the very serious menace which the economic reconstruction of Empire-resources and Empire-industries seem to offer to India.

Although so far the only change in the British economic policy that has been publicly announced is the abandonment of the old principles of Free Trade and the adoption of Protection in the shape of Imperial Preference, this is clearly not the only revolution which is in contemplation in regard to the economic principles and policy of the Empire. What this contemplated revolution is, was foreshadowed in the *Times* by the authors of the "Elements of Reconstruction" to which I have already referred.

The central plea of these neo-Imperialist economists is that the days of small "individualistic" businesses are gone, just as the days of small isolated sovereign states are practically gone in world-politics where the future of small nationalities lies in their ability to combine and confederate themselves into big Empires. National industries, to thrive and hold their own in world-competitions, must be combined and amalgamated into big concerns commanding large capital and organisation. This is the first step. This step is already being taken by many cognate concerns. Because, "big businesses, progressive methods, and scientific research come together. Syndicating businesses and organising scientific education and research are two aspects of the same job."

For a long time past, an increasing number of British politicians and economists have been trying to induce their people and their Government to pursue the advanced industrial policy of Germany for the preservation and revival of their national industries. The war has pushed this school to the front; for the war has fully revealed the superiority of German methods to the British methods. Germany combined superior technological and scientific education and research with industrial works. The same thing must be done by the British also.

> "Those who are attacking the problem of the industrial re-organisation of the Empire and those who are working for educational reconstruction must join hands."

In plain English, it means that big business amalgamations must be formed with immense resources in money and men at their command. These combines will be in a position to maintain adequate scientific establishment furnished with well-equipped laboratories for research work cognate to their particular industry. They will be able to keep pace with progressive inventions and discoveries with such establishments at their back. In the next place, with the large capital at their back these combines will be able to deal with labour in such a way as will make strikes and lock-outs and other troubles more or less impossible. Because they will be able to retain their men for exceptionally long periods, train many of them specially, and pension the old men off; and they will do all this, with no pretention to philanthropy but because it will pay. As those writers point out:—

> "But no small hundred-thousand-pound concern can afford to do anything of the sort; it works on a narrower basis for two immediate ends. A chemical

industry on an Imperial scale can, on the other hand, do things on a far wider basis, can work for larger and remoter advantages, and turn its vast profits far more directly to the enduring benefit of the community. It can plan such a liberal and comprehensive treatment of labour as no smaller employer can attempt. The minor employer deals with his men by the hour, day, or job; he has to take them as they come "out of the unknown" to him; he is unable to treat them generously as they age; he is powerless to help their children; indeed, to do his duty in any way beyond the immediate business in hand. But a nationalised industry can see the life of labour as a whole, and can deal with its own section of organised labour not through a mere string of isolated jobs, snatch-profit occasions, and petty disputes, but as a scheme of lives; can guarantee ease presently in return for energy now, and can formulate and realise big, thorough, efficient, economical, and racially beneficial schemes of education, training, selection, direction, and research."

But these huge business amalgamations may be a possible danger to a democratic State. The tendency of these will be to run the Government in the interest of the capitalists. This is a thing which has no chance of being acceptable to the vast body of British working-men who have got sufficient political power in their hands to turn out any Government they like, and in case this is resisted, to hurl the country in a bloody revolution.

These Imperialist writers are fully conscious of all this. And they propose, therefore, a compromise between the working classes and the capitalist interests which their school of Imperialism practically represent. The British working-men, like the majority of their class all over Europe, are more or less Socialists.

For a long time past this Socialism has been very largely influencing European political and economic evolution. The central demand of Socialism has been that neither land nor "works," by which is meant large organisation for national industries, should be owned by private profiteers but should be claimed for the nation by the State which represents the life and authority of the totality of a people. While it has not as yet been fully accepted anywhere, there has been clear movement of what is known as State Socialism in almost every European country during the last decade or two. Though the late war may have, as the authors of the "Elements of Reconstruction" seem to think, marked the "end of the Socialist movement," even they have been forced to recognise that Socialism has achieved great and abiding results in that it has completely killed the old doctrine of *laissez faire.* "But the movement combined general ideas of the utmost sanity with methods of utter impracticability; and while the sounder elements of the Socialistic proposal have so passed into the general consciousness as to be no longer distinctive, its rejected factors shrivel and perish as things completely judged, and its name becomes a shelter for "rebels and faddists."

So that, while on the one hand, the bulk of reasonable men in the Empire have come over to the primary Socialist assertion that food production, transport, all the big industrialism are matters not for the profit-seeking of private ownership, but for public administration, it has also come to the completest realisation that it is impossible to wrench these services suddenly from the hands that control them now. We cannot cut to-morrow off from yesterday; the world will be of the same men. Without any preachment or propaganda we all find ourselves to-day drifted into a virtual agreement upon the reasonable course of economic development. It is development towards nationalisation: so far we go with the Socialist, but it is development not by the Socialist's panacea of "expropriation" at all, but by amalgamation, by co-ordination and co-operation, by the bringing the State into partnership, and an increasing partnership, in the big businesses that result from these amalgamations, by developing the crude beginnings of the "controlled establishment," by the *quid pro quo* of profit-sharing and control in the national interest in exchange for the national credit and a helpful tariff.

It will be observed that this is practically a repetition in different wording and in another context of the policy of the TIMES-MILNER School noticed in a previous page which pleaded for direct State action in the work of the economic "development" of the depending Empire. And it is just here that the new ideals of Imperial economic reconstruction offer so serious a menace to us.

The war has largely revolutionised the character of British policy; but in nothing has this revolution been so complete as in regard to economic and industrial matters. In the first place the marvellous successes of the operations of the enemy during the earlier months, indeed, for the earlier years of the struggle revealed the close connection that German national industries, specially the chemical researches, originally started for obvious industrial objects, had with the manufacture of munition of war. Great Britain had, therefore, to initiate similar researches both at home and in her dependencies, particularly in India, with a view to organise improved methods of the production of munitions and other necessaries of the army and the navy, on the one hand; and on the other, to acquire and temporarily "nationalise," so to say, many of the great industrial plants owned by private capitalists, for the purpose of making munitions. Practically, therefore, the entire industrial organisation of the country was temporarily converted into a huge department of the State. This was, though forced by the necessity of the war-situation, a very valuable experiment of very far-reaching consequences in a new form of State-Socialism beyond the imagination of the most ardent Socialist.

The war did another thing also. The scarcity of food due to the stoppage of the continental trade of Great Britain necessitated the organisation of measures for food-economy on the one hand, and the production of food-products in the country under direct State control, on the other. The authors of the "ELEMENTS OF RECONSTRUCTION," from which I have already drawn largely to show the trend and nature of the new Imperial economic ideal and policy, have prominently noticed this new development:

> "It is not one of the least compensations for this war that it has necessitated experiments upon an otherwise impossible scale in the handling and rationing of the people's food and drink, and upon the conversion of private into quasi-public businesses. There has been haste and no doubt there has been waste and a considerable variety of incidental inaccuracies and abuses, favouritism, jobbery, the wrong man in this place and the crooked man in that, but on the whole this series of improvised "nation-

alisations" is full of suggestion and encouragement for the more deliberate and permanent readjustments that must be made after the war. The most striking demonstration has been of the practicability of the State coming as the food-buyer and distributor, and of the great possibilities of control and participation that this opens out to us, first, of the already very extensively syndicated popular provision-trade of the country, and secondly, of the cultivator. The state can step in here with a minimum of social disturbance. It need expropriate no body, it need confiscate nothing, it leaves the landlord his acres, the farmer his farm, the wholesaler his warehouse, and the retailer his shop; but, on the one hand, it can insist upon certain standards of the quality, wholesomeness and cheapness, and on the other certain standards of cultivation. The great advantage of the quasi-public big business is that the profit the State-partner seeks is not a dividend but the public welfare. It can afford to buy even at a loss a crop which is socially beneficial, it can afford to sell even at a loss product which is wholesome or socially stimulating. Its aim is a highly cultivated country and a well-fed, energetic population. Big business, and particularly State business, means wide views and distant ends, and they are attainable in no other way.

There are others also whose views on these subjects have been more or less revolutionised by the experiences of the war. Among these Sir Chiozza Money, at one time regarded as a great authority on economic matters among advanced British Liberals, may be counted. He published a scheme in 1916 which practically supports the new economic policy advocated by the authors of the "Elements of Reconstruction," and has been approvingly cited by them. Sir Chiozza Money's scheme proposes, roughly speaking, that the "State by co-ordinating the present wholesalers and distributing agencies, should buy all the food in the country and hand it to retailers. It would buy first the national produce, and this it would buy with a view to developing the highest and most beneficial forms of cultivation. It would then supplement this supply by buying through the Colonial Governments and importing the Colonial output. Finally it would, if necessary, complete its needs by buying in the cheapest foreign market. It would, of course, buy at three price levels, and it would in effect subsidise the home grower, who would have as his encouragement not a protective tariff but a bonus price. And the cost of this encouragement would fall not upon the poorer sort of consumer, as a tariff would do, but upon the general community, which would be profiting by the security and prosperity of agriculture and by the increased national safety to which a well-maintained agriculture conduces.

All these things have very important bearings upon our own economic future. Like the Government of the United Kingdom the Government of India also had to organise whatever industries we had in the country, for war purposes; and a Munitions Board with Sir Thomas Holland as President, and some leading British merchants in the country as members, was formed here. In their attempt to organise munition-making here, Sir T. Holland's Board had to make a very careful survey of our natural resources, both agricultural and mineral. The experiences thus gained will be bound to be of very great value in the coming economic reconstruction of the

Empire. All this will be bound to be utilised very largely for the new economic exploitation which will have to be undertaken first for the revival of British and Empire trade which had been woefully disorganised by the war; and secondly, for meeting the heavy financial obligations which the last five years of war have placed upon the British nation; and thirdly, for devising means for the exclusion of the erstwhile enemies of the Empire for the Empire-markets. Though President Wilson had declared that there must be no after-war economic war upon the German people or their allies in the last war, the general trend of British and Imperial opinion on this subject, has as yet held out no manner of hope whatsoever that the Europeon Allies of Dr. Wilson will readily accept at least this one of his historic Fourteen Points.

XIV

MUNITION BOARD AND INDUSTRIAL COMMISSION

In the next place, as in the United Kingdom so also here in India, our Government had to organise to some extent measures of food and cloth control. This has so far been done only in the matter of food and cloth distribution, and specially in regard to price. But attempts have already been made to take stock of both food and clothes stored in the country; and more particularly in the regulation of imports and exports. All this, however, has worked, it seems, somewhat differently from what happened in the United Kingdom. This official "control" has not, in any case, helped to reduce the price either of food or clothing to the poor people. All that has practically happened is the entrance of the Government in the field of private commercial enterprise, as "controller;" and it may gradually lead to the introduction of the principle of profit-sharing partnership between the Government in India and foreign and possibly even indigenous capitalist exploiters. And it is just this which we all must carefully mark, note and inwardly digest.

And it should also be noted that the principal recommendations of the Industrial Commission also seem to clear the way for this new economic exploitation. Sir Sankaran Nair has fully grasped the significance of these recommendations and has noted them in his Note of Dissent from the Government of India's Despatch on the Reforms Proposals, dated March 5, 1919:

"We know now, that there are Trade Commissioners whose business it is to find out the natural resources and facilities for trade—

> English trade in particular—that exist in the country. The results of their observations are to be made the basis of expert advice as to the best mode of utilising those resources in the interests of English trade. It is true that the information would be equally available to the Indian public, but we know that it is the commercial organisations in England that would be able to utilize them."

Hitherto, the Government in India pursued the policy of *laissez faire*, following the dominant political and economic philosophy of the British nation from the second half of the last century, and did not directly engage itself in any large measure of State socialism, especially in the matter of our industries. All that it did was to offer protection to foreign exploiters, and in special circumstances give them facilities through the administration of land-laws and rail-road construction and the granting or securing mining leases that have always been subject to the sanction of the Government of India; and, in the case of the Assam tea industry, by especially favourable labour laws. A good deal of this was, however, left more to the discretion of local officials whose social relations with the European trading and mercantile community offered peculiar facilities to the latter to exploit these relations for their personal profits in connection with their business enterprise.

It was Lord Curzon, as we have already pointed out, who for the first time realised the supreme value of this British capitalist exploitation to the British Indian Empire; and his Lordship openly declared the intimate and organic relation that exists or ought to exist, between administration and exploitation in this country.

His lordship maintained that it is a part of the duty of the Government in India "to hold out the hand of friendship to industrial or commercial enterprises, to endeavour, by careful study, to understand its conditions, and to secure its loyal co-operation." This was the motive of the establishment of the new Department of Commerce and Industry in 1905, with a special and high-paid officer to work it.

The object of this new Department was the acquisition and dissemination of industrial information, the introduction of new and the stimulation of existing industries. For this purpose provincial Directors of Industries were appointed, who were advised by a board of officials and business men; and with their help and of a competent staff of experts, the Directors were to "pioneer new industries and to experiment in improved methods and demonstrate their application to certain existing industries on a commercial scale."

This new policy, initiated by Lord Curzon, received, however, scant support from the Liberal Government in London when they came to power soon after his Lordship's retirement from India; and the "essential feature of experiment and demonstration by Government agency on a commercial scale" entirely failed to secure the approval of the new Secretary of State for India. Lord Morley declared that the "results of the attempts to create new industries were not of a character to remove his doubts as to the utility of State effort in this direction, unless it were strictly limited to industrial instruction and avoided the semblance of a commercial value." The office of the Director of Industries was, however, retained, but Lord Crewe who succeeded Lord Morley as Indian Secretary, defined his duties as follows (Report Industrial Commission, p. 79).

1. to collect information as to existing industries, their needs and the possibility of improving them or of introducing new industries;

2. to carry out and direct experiments connected with such enquiries:
3. to keep in touch with local manufacturers, to bring the results of his experiments to their notice and to obtain their co-operation in the conduct of operations on a commercial scale;
4. to supervise the training of students; and
5. to advise Government with regard to technical matters involving legislation.

"Even after Lord Crewe's despatch," continues the Report, "the Government of India seemed to be in doubt as to how far they would be justified in sanctioning proposals for demonstration plants, financial assistance and other forms of direct aid to industries. Their desire to move in these matters, which had not so far reached the stage of active fulfilment, had received a decided set-back. The difficulties were increased by the fact that they had neither the organisation nor the equipment to give effect even to the comparatively limited policy sanctioned by Lord Morley. It was not, however, till some time after the outbreak of war that they resolved to examine the question in a comprehensive way, and to that end appointed our Commission."

This Commission has recommended a closer and more organic association of Government with the industrial and commercial development of the country than in the past. With this end in view it has recommended, among other things, the organisation of an Indian Chemical Service which will entirely devote itself to the pursuit of research in the domain of industrial chemistry or chemical industries. The results of all research work, either by the Chemical or any other scientific department connected with the Government Department of Commerce and Industry, should be regarded as the property of the Government;

and the decision of the expediency of publishing these must rest with the "controlling authorities." But care should be taken that this in no way precludes the confidential communication of any such results that may not be published for general information to "persons who may be interested in it, or who may be in a position to make use of it advantageously." The Commission further recommend that the Government Department of Scientific Research in relation to industry, should always be ready to help "pioneer industries or existing industries undertaken under new conditions' free of all charges; and these industries should be able also to "have research work taken up on their behalf in Government laboratories, without charge."

Another important recommendation of the commission is in regard to the acquisition of land for industrial undertakings. Para 199 of the Report discusses the present situation in this matter, and may be profitably quoted here :—

"Many witnesses, representing both large and small interests, complained of the handicap imposed on industrial enterprise by difficulties in obtaining land for the sites of factories and other industrial concerns, and the surface rights of mines, in cases where mineral rights are not the property of Government. These difficulties are said to lie, first, in the trouble experienced in obtaining a good title, in view of the complicated system under which land is held in certain parts of the country, especially in Bengal, and in the absence (in some provinces) of an authentic record of rights; second, in provincial laws, designed to prevent the expropriation of tenant-interests; and last, in the attitude of landholders, who are too apt to exploit unduly the necessities of an industrialist whose choice of the site for a new venture is

> limited by consideration of transport, water supply, etc., while he is still more fettered when he desires to extend an existing factory. There are also often cases where the land required belongs to a large number of small owners, and when any one of these declines to sell, his refusal may render the consent of the rest useless. We have also received complaints regarding the obstinate and dilatory attitude often taken up by landholders in negotiating transfers."

This matter was carefully considered, we are told, by the Bombay Advisory Committee, who suggested the following formula as a guide to Local Governments in the exercise of their discretion on behalf of an industrial concern:

> When such acquisition is indispensable to the development of the industry, and......the development of the industry itself is in the interests of the general public.

Sir T. Holland's Commission recommend that this formula may be accepted with the following modifications—

"The Local Government may acquire land compulsorily from private owners on behalf of an industrial concern, when it is satisfied—

1. that the industry itself will, on reaching a certain stage of development, be in the interest of the general public ;
2. that there are no reasonable prospects of the industry reaching such a stage of development without the acquisition proposed ;
3. that the proposed acquisition entails as little inconvenience to private rights as is possible, consistently with meeting the needs of the industry. In this connection we wish to draw particular attention to the desirability of avoiding, as far as possible, the acquisition of areas largely covered by residential buildings.

Sir T. Holland's Commission add further that *when Government considers an industrial undertaking deserving of substantial assistance in other ways at the public expense, especially when it adopts such a course as an alternative to carrying on the industry itself, there seems no reason why land, when necessary, should not be acquired compulsorily.*

The Italics are mine. This recommendation of the Indian Industrial Commission shows clearly the trends of the coming industrial and economic policy of the Government of India, which must, we think, to be correctly appreciated, be read along with the bolder and more unreserved, because un-official, statement of the authors of the "Elements of Reconstruction" to which pointed attention has been repeatedly drawn in foregoing pages.

Chapter XIV of the Report of the Industrial Commission is of special importance in this connection. It deals with a form of State Socialism which has very strange affinity with the new form of it suggested in the "Elements of Reconstruction." This chapter indicates "in somewhat greater detail *the special necessity which exists in India for direct Government participation in the initiation and improvement of industries*..." In Para 212, the Report deals with "Industries of national importance" in this connection, which says:

> In our chapter on the industrial deficiencies of India, (Ch. IV) we have given some account of the work which will have to be done to place India on a firm basis of economic self-sufficiency and of self-defence; and it is clear that, from this point of view, there are strong arguments for a policy of direct Government assistance in respect of essential new industries.
>
> We contemplate that only in exceptional circumstances will Government itself carry

> on industrial operations on a commercial scale; but it is necessary to establish and maintain Government factories for the manufacture of lethal munitions, and to exercise some degree of control over private factories upon which dependence will be placed for the supply of military necessities.
>
> This, in most cases, could be obtained in return for guarantees to take over a definite proportion of the output, and should be exercised only to ensure that adequate provision is made to meet the prospective demands of the country in times of war.

But the partnership of the State with private industrial enterprises will not be confined, if the recommendations of the Commission are accepted, only to this particular class of industry with which Government Military Stores and Munitions Departments may be intimately related. For the Commissioners say:

> Besides industries essential to the safety of the

country in time of war, we have mentioned others which will be of considerable economic importance and add to the industrial strength of the country in peace time.

And, while the actual inception of these undertakings will usually be a matter for private enterprise, and the necessary assistance in regard to these may be given by the Provincial Department of Industries, "they will sometimes be of such importance to the country generally, and require employment by Government of so costly and specialised an agency to work out the preliminary data, that it will be beyond the scope of any Local Government to do all that is needed." And in these cases the Imperial Government must come to the assistance of private enterprise.

The Industrial Commission has not gone the length of suggesting that in the matter of these industries of national importance, as they call them, the state should enter into any profit-sharing partnership with them; but it may be noted that they do imagine "instances," where the "conditions may be such that the expense of production will always exceed the cost at which articles of similar quality can be imported, and in such cases, the industry can only be maintained by the grant of direct financial assistance or by the indirect operation of protective duties; but in either case, the burden will really fall upon the Indian taxpayer.

I have no desire to discuss the recommendations of the Industrial Commission here; and if I have at all referred to some of these, it is only to indicate that there is a suspicious family-likeness between the economic policy of the dominant school of present-day British Imperialism, as represented by the *Times* and Lord Milner, and the policy indicated in the Report of our Industrial Commission. And this fact should be borne in mind by every Indian politician and economist seeking to solve the problem of our economic reconstruction.

XV

THE WAR-DEBT—HOW TO MEET IT?

THE new economic policy of the Empire, namely, the energetic exploitation of the immense economic resources of the tropical and "dependent" Empire, as the *Times* has so aptly described it, by a system of profit-sharing partnership between the State and private capitalist amalgamations, has, in fact, been forced upon Imperial statesmanship by the imperious obligations which the last five years of war have placed upon the British Exchequer. A high financial authority, Mr. Edgar Crammond, in a speech to the Institute of Bankers, London, estimated the total cost of the last war at 52 thousand million sterling; of this more than 25 thousand millions had to be borne by the Allies. "There had been nothing," he said, "approaching this destruction of capital wealth in the history of the world, and this stupendous conflict had produced the greatest economic revolution of which there was any record."

On February 1st, 1919, the net amount of British national debt was 6099 millions sterling, and the interest and sinking fund charges might be estimated at 350 millions per annum. The pre-war national debt of the United Kingdom was 650 millions sterling, and the annual charge on it was 24 and half millions only. So it will be seen that the war has added 5450 millions to the national debt, and 325 millions to the annual charge.

But after the war, the British Peace Budget will probably stand at 825 millions. In 1913–14 the cost of the Imperial Government was 198 millions. How to meet this increased demand is the most acute financial problem just now before the Imperial Government. The Budget for 1919 had been built practically upon the balance of which the sudden termination of the war in 1918 left in the treasury. As the Calcutta *Statesman* pointed out, the British Budget for 1919 was worked upon very misleading figures. For instance, the "revenue" actually included 300 millions sterling of deferred payment under the previous year's Excess Profits taxation, and a first instalment of 200 millions derived from the realisation of war-assets, the sale of which was rendered possible by the early conclusion of peace. On the other hand, the departmental expenditure is kept down to the extent of 254 millions by similar realisations, which do not appear as "revenue" at all. Thus the nation was still living in a large measure on the results of expenditure which it authorised during the war period, and the *Statesman* opines that for some years to come it will appear for the same reason to be better off than it really is.

The stern fact is that the Imperial Exchequer will be put to very great strain for a pretty long series of years to come to meet the heavy financial obligations which the war has placed upon it. Some attempt will, no doubt, be made to recoup part at least of the war-debt by the indemnity claim from the beaten enemy; but considering the condition of the enemy-countries and the general attitude of their populations, particularly of Germany from which the largest war-indemnity is claimed, it is exceedingly doubtful if these hopes will be substantially materialised.

Indeed, British politicians and financiers seem to be quite wide awake about this matter; and from the commencement of the war various committees have been at work seeking to discover the most effective means of meeting the obligations of the war on the one hand, and of practically killing continental, and particularly German, competition in home and Colonial trade after the war.

XVI

"EMPIRE RESOURCES DEVELOPMENT COMMITTEE"

ALL through the five years of war British imperialists and financiers had been seriously engaged in tackling this question of finding a way out of the grave financial and commercial crisis which was likely to be brought about by it. As early as the middle of 1917, a non-official, but very influential committee was at work seeking to solve this problem. It is known as the "Empire Resources Development Committee." Mr. H. Wilson Fox, M. P. was the Secretary, and Sir Starr Jameson of the Jameson Raid fame, (since dead) was Chairman of this Committee, which counted among its members Lord Islington, the late Under-Secretary for India, Sir Arthur

Lawley, one-time Governor of Madras, Lord Grey, Mr. Ian Macpherson, the present Secretary for Ireland, Sir Henry Page Croft, the leader of the newly-formed National Party in the British Parliament, and a good many other prominent British politicians and Imperialists of the *Times*-Milner school. Mr. John H. Harris, writing to the *Westminister Gazette*, in May 1917, said that this Committee " has come into existence with the laudable object of providing the British public with an easy method of paying the war-debt."

> The Committee (said Mr. Harris) is a private body, but its membership includes several ministers of the Crown and other gentlemen ......the driving force on the Committee is that of the Rhodesian Chartered Company; Sir Starr Jameson, President of that company, is the Chairman of the "Empire Resources Development Committee," Mr. Wilson Fox, another director is honorary

secretary, whilst the Rhodesian conception of colonisation is writ large upon every one of its proposals as explained by Mr. Wilson Fox.

The manifesto of the Committee is fairly innocuous, because it is limited to laudable generalities, but the speeches of the honorary secretary disclose the whole programme in all its absurdity and crudeness. *The objective thus disclosed is that of exploiting the natural resources of the Dependencies in order to obtain "hundreds of millions sterling per annum" for the war debt, by securing these virgin assets as "Crown Estates," to be worked by monopoly syndicates, to whom would be accorded "special positions" in return for a participation in the profits by the mother country.*

And the most significant part of the programme of the Committee, as pointed by Mr. Harris, is that

> *It is not proposed, for the present, to apply these proposals to the Dominions, but to the crown Colonies, Protectorates and to India. The oil palms of West Africa and the cocoanut palms of the South Seas, India, Ceylon, and the Straits Settlements are the first raw products to be attacked.*

The *Daily News* (London) described this scheme as "dangerous," particularly, because "it was said to have the support of five Ministers of the Crown, and was endeavouring to commit the State to a policy of Colonisation involving (to use the words of Lord Henry Cavendish Bentink, M. P.) a flagrant departure from the best rock principle upon which the British Empire is founded—that Government should exist for the good of the governed."

XVII

REVIVING THE OLD "CONGO REGIME"

THE Annual Report of the Anti-Slavery and Aborigines Protection Society (1916—'17) put in on record that

'The proposals of Mr. Wilson Fox, M.P., Hon. Secretary of the Empire Development Committee, have in them every one of the vicious principles of the old Congo regime—State exploitation, monopoly vegetable products, and the diversion of revenue from the colony which, if carried out, cannot fail to reduce the native to servitude.' (Quoted by *New India* May 30, 1917).

Lord Henry (quoted by the same paper, evidently from the report of the annual meeting of the Anti-Slavery Society) asked: "Are they (*i.e.*) the natives of South Africa, to be dispossessed of their property and treated as mere wage-earners and labourers? This question is assuming a character of the very greatest importance. *There is no doubt about it—a movement is on foot in this country to take away from the natives* their rights as citizens of the British Empire"

Mr. Morel explained the project of the "Empire Resources Development Committee," as one which implies "a partnership between the State and financial corporations seeking profits for investors of capital."

"In that system (he said) and in that partnership, all that past Colonial tragedies of the world have their root. For Mr. Wilson Fox the native is merely an undeveloped national asset. All West Africa, in his view, is State land. But that land belongs to the native communities of British West Africa and no one else—by treaty, by solemn obligations, by hundreds of agreements entered into by the Government of this country. It would mean converting not one treaty, but hundreds of treaties, into scraps of paper. It would be comparable only to the system introduced by Leopold in the Belgian Congo,......"

All these criticism seems to be fully justified by a mere glance at the "aims and proposal" of the Committee, as appeared from a statement published by it in the early part of 1917. The opening words of it are:

"We, the undersigned realising the immense latent resources of the Empire, and the possibility of developing this great and varied wealth for State-purposes under State auspices, and so lifting from the peoples of the Empire the burdens caused by the War, have formed ourselves into a Committee for the following purposes:—

These purposes include *(a)* the advocacy of

the conservation for the benefit of the Empire of such natural resources as are, or may come, under the ownership or control of the Imperial Dominions or Indian Governments *(b)* The development of selected resources of the Empire under such conditions as will give to the State an adequate share of these proceeds.

The statement next publishes some of the suggestions that have been made to it, among which occur the following, namely, that " the State should control the production of vegetable oils and fats raised in the tropical possessions of the Crown ;" and it observes :—

> The facilities at the disposal of the State are obviously such as no individual or corporation can command—unlimited credit, unique source of information, power of legislation, special means of rewarding its servants, and power to conclude arrangements with foreign Governments.

And, it is suggested that those facilities should be utilised for the exploitation of the natural resources of the Dependencies with a view to lift the burden of the War from the peoples of the Empire.

To work this plan out the Government will have to appoint an Imperial Board of Controllers or Directors. It should be composed of not more than twenty prominent business men, with whom should be associated a small number of leading Civil Servants.

The committee divided State enterprises under their scheme into two classes: (i) Undertaking which the State proposes to develop *ab initio* on its own account; and (ii) Existing businesses or trades in which the State may elect to participate. How the second class of undertaking are to be organised has been indicated as follows: The state may proceed in this class of enterprise—

(*a*) by buying out all existing interests for cash.

(*b*) by arranging to employ individuals or corporations already engaged in the business, under such conditions as would ensure to them a prosperous future, while securing to the State ownership and control:

(*c*) by federating all interests concerned, possibly on a share or debenture basis, under arrangements which gave to the State ultimate control, and a considerable share of the profits—say one half—the State in return giving assistance and facilities for the extension of the business, particularly in connection with the raising of further capital.

As regards the effect of this great economic development upon the course of political freedom or responsible Government in the subject or dependent countries, it may be clearly realised from the following remarks of Mr. John H. Harris in the *Westminister Gazette*, already referred to in the above:

"The third cardinal principle which these proposals would violate," says Mr. Harris, "...the supreme necessity of recognising indigenous law and custom, especially in so far as they affect land ownership. It is useless to say that under this scheme Mr. Wilson Fox does not aim at the expropriation of native state ownership of land. It is impossible to import any other meaning than expropriation into the following:

"There is no reason to suppose that these territories will ever receive any large measure of local self-government, and there will be the less difficulty in regarding them mainly from the standpoint of estates of the Crown, which should be developed for the general benefit of the Empire, and at the same time of their native inhabitants."

And again:

The adoption of sane, just, and practical views in regard to native ownership of land and native labour is above all essential."

"There is no need to waste time over sentimental nonsense about the welfare of the natives: there has never yet been a system of exploitation which did not loudly assert that its main object was the good of the native, who, by the way, detests sentiment, and only asks for justice."

XVIII

LORD BALFOUR OF BURLEIGH'S COMMITTEE

IT would be a mistake to think that the "Empire Resources Development Committee" of Sir Starr Jameson and Mr. Wilson Fox had no formal official backing from the Imperial Government. It will be remembered that an official Committee was appointed with exactly similar aims and objects, namely, to examine and report upon the means of the economic development of the Empire with a view to preserve and increase the trade and commerce of the Empire and organise measures for after-war trade, so that in the future the enemy nations might not be in a position to hurt the Empire in these respects. Lord Bal-

K

four of Burleigh was the Chairman of this Committee.

It should also be noted that the Dominions Royal Commission practically support the suggestion of the Empire Resources Development Committee in the matter of the formation of an Imperial Development Board. The Dominions Royal Commission declared that

> "It was vital that the Empire should, as far as possible, be placed in a position which would enable it to resist any pressure which a foreign Power or group of Powers could exercise in time of peace or war, in virtue of a control of raw materials and commodities essential to its well-being.

A Committee appointed to enquire into post-war trade affairs submitted a Report unanimously recommending:

1. In the light of experience gained during the War, we consider that special steps must be taken to stimulate the production

of foodstuffs, raw materials, and manufactured articles within the Empire wherever the expansion of production is possible and economically desirable for the safety and welfare of the Empire as a whole.

2. We, therefore, recommend that His Majesty's Government should now declare that adherence to the principle that preference should be accorded to the products and manufactures of the British Overseas Dominions in respect of any Customs Duties now or here-after to be imposed on imports into the United Kingdom.

3. Further, it will, in our opinion, be necessary to take into early consideration, as one of the methods of achieving the above objects the desirability of establishing a wider range of Customs Duties, which would be remitted or reduced on the products and manufactures of the Empire, and which would from the basis

of commercial treaties with Allied and Neutral Powers.

It will thus be seen that while our active politicians were quarrelling over such trivialities as to whether we should or should not accept the Montagu-Chelmsford reforms, and whether we shall declare them as worthy of our grateful acknowledgment or deserving of our rejection unless substantially modified, the leaders of the Empire were engaged in the far more vital questions concerning the development of the resources of the Empire in the interest of the capitalist enterprises of the United Kingdom and the Dominions, paving silently and insidiously the way to the gradual materialisation of the ideal and policy foreshadowed ten years ago by the *Times*.

XIX

SOCIAL INFLUENCES IN EXPLOITATION

I HAVE already indicated the various forces that are at work just now aiming at the relentless exploitation of the natural resources of what the *Times* described ten years ago as the "Dependent" Empire, including India. The need of this exploitation is also very great; for it is at least one of the means by which the British Exchequer may hope to relieve the financial pressure due to the war. And the method which will be adopted, if the counsels of the dominant school of current British Imperialism find acceptance with the responsible rulers of the Empire, which seems to be very likely, will be "profit-sharing state-partnership in private capitalist amalgamations." It is high time that we clearly realised what this will mean to our own economic future.

As Sir Sankaran Nair frankly pointed out in his Note of Dissent, "the general policy of the subordination of Indian to British commercial interests has continued from the time of the East India Company to this day." But hitherto the Government offered only indirectly what assistance British capitalist interests required for our economic exploitation. More frequently, the main help was received from individual officials in more or less intimate social relations with the representative of British commercial interests in the country. In most cases, the laws and regulations make no invidious distinctions between Indians and non-Indians in these matters. For instance, the law regulating the grant of the lease of mines or Government lands, or even private-owned lands favourable for industrial enterprises as tea or coffee, is fair and impartial. There is absolutely no provision in this law for favouring non-Indian applicants for long term leases to the prejudice of Indian applicants. But, in some parts of the country, the heads of the district administrations have to sanction these leases. There are good reasons for this restriction also; because free grant of lease in these cases might lead to various abuses, and prevent their proper utilisation for the production of valuable industrial crops. All this cannot be denied. At the same time, these discretions given to European officers lead sometimes in practice to differential treatment of applications for lease as between Indians and non-Indians. I do not say that this is always deliberately done. Wherever these things happen, they are the natural result of social intimacies, which work unconsciously in the mind of the official. In other matters also, Indian commercial enterprises suffer through these reasons. The waggon-supply in almost every Indian railway has been, more or less, at the disposal of the superior railway officials, who stand in close social relations with the non-Indian merchants and traders; the latter consequently get advantages, sometimes, which are not open to their Indian rivals. These social influences have hitherto worked prejudicially to Indian enterprise, and have helped the exploitation of our natural resources and extensive markets by foreign merchants and capitalists. But the Government had no connection with it. Sometimes the Government did legislate on the supply of Indian labour to some foreign capitalist enterprises; as they did, for instance, in 1858 on Labour Contracts between a cooly and the employer of large labour contingents, where the maintenance of regular labour supply was found essential for the protection of the works that employed them; or again in 1881, for the special benefit of the tea enterprise in Assam. This last Act—the Assam Cooly Act—was characterized by even so sober a publicist as the late Hon. Kristodas Pal, then a member of the Viceroy's Legislative Council, as the Assam Slave Act. But these special cases apart, the Government, as Government, has hitherto had no connection with foreign capitalist or commercial exploitation in this country.

But, if this new economic policy of "profit-sharing state-partnership with private capitalist amalgamations" be once adopted by the Imperial Government, then the process of foreign, and particularly British capitalist exploitation of our large natural resources, our teeming and frugal labour, and our extensive market, will go on more vigorously than ever, under the protection of the Government of India and with the help of the extensive administrative agencies at the command of the Indian executive.

XX

"MOBILISATION OF INDIA'S AGRICULTURAL RESOURCES"

A SIGNIFICANT article published in the autumn of 1918 in the *Times* suggesting the "mobilisation of India's Agricultural Resources," throws considerable light on this aspect of the problem we have been discussing.

In view of anticipated world scarcity of food, the *Times* proposed that "the mobilisation of India's agricultural resources must be directed by the Government of the country, and not left to individual enterprise." To this end, "general and drastic action will be required;" and "the area of industrial crops must be curtailed, and ten, twenty, or even thirty million acres diverted to the production of food."

> "On the average about three acres will yield a ton, so that given favourable season, the surplus of food, which India sends to Europe, could, for a single year, be doubled or even trebled at the cost of curtailing the supply of raw materials and forcing Asia to wear old clothes in order that Europe may not starve."

And the *Times* thinks that "it is quite within the competence of the existing land-administration" to do it. "If,..., plain orders are issued in the spring and measures are taken to ensure an adequate supply of seed and capital, the result will be seen in increased supplies of maize, millets and pulses coming forward in the following autumn, and of wheat, gram and barley a few months later, in time to reach Europe at the critical period when it is waiting for the northern harvests to begin."

"A word of warning must be offered by way of conclusion. If the War Cabinet should unhappily be driven to the decision that India's peasants must be mobilised in the interests of the world's food, the operation must be so conducted as to afford no scope for a cry of exploitation. The peasant will be asked to sacrifice his independence; that sacrifice ought to suffice, and he should not be required to undertake increased financial liability. In other words, the curtailment of industrial crops must be accompanied by a guarantee of minimum prices for good grains sufficient to ensure that the peasant shall not be a loser, and that politicians or agitators shall be given no grounds for a charge that India is paying dearly to provide Europe's food. Given this condition, it is not unreasonable that the area which is already a reserve against scarcity of food

> in India, should be claimed in the interests of that civilisation in whose benefits India shares."

Hitherto the production of food grains has been left entirely to the Indian peasants themselves. They are free to raise any crops they like, whether for the production of food grains or of raw materials for industrial purposes. About the middle of the last century, the indigo planters in Bengal tried to force the Bengal peasantry to produce indigo at the cost of rice and other food grains. They were, however, in no way identified with the Government. Whatever help they received from the district officials in securing forced labour for their factories, was due to their chromatic kinship and social relations with individual members of the Administration. The Government, as the Government, had no interest whatever in this economic enterprise. Still, how much did the poor peasantry suffer may be judged from the fact that six millions of them ceased to cultivate not only indigo but all food crops also to secure their release from the yoke of the planters.

Even before our own eyes we have had more recent experiences of the results of agricultural operations conducted in Behar by British capital and through British agency. Recent disturbances in Champaran have only repeated the experiences of the indigo-troubles in Nadia, Jessore and the 24 Pergunnas and other districts. And these experiences offer no encouragement to us to take any optimistic view of the future of the Indian peasantry if the Government of India undertakes the work of the "mobilisation of India's agricultural resources," as has been suggested by the "Times"; and if the policy of "forcing Asia to wear old clothes in order that Europe may not starve" be courageously carried out.

The ostensible plea of the policy, suggested by the "*Times*," was based on the apprehension of "a world-scarcity of food." How far this apprehension is real and the need of providing against it is urgent, are questions which the "*Times*," is pleased to leave to the decision of the War Cabinet. The War Cabinet may, however, be easily induced to accept the significant suggestion of the "*Times*," for other reasons also. And, as these other reasons may not justify the general and drastic action recommended by the "*Times*," the Cabinet may find in this apprehended world-scarcity, an excellent excuse for the adoption of this pólicy with a more or less clear conscience. And it is just here that the real danger of this mischievous suggestion comes in.

Economically, this principle of compulsion is fundamentally wrong. The "economic man" always produces that which pays him most. The Indian peasant, particularly in Bengal, has, since some years past, been curtailing the production of food grains with a view to increase the production of jute, for instance; simply because jute pays him more. The market for jute is mainly foreign. Great Britain, and Germany and Austria more progressively had been the principal buyers of Indian jute. The present war has seriously interfered with the export of this precious fibre and has seriously affected the price of this article. The result has been a return of the peasants to the cultivation of food grains that fetches more value than jute. If the end of the war should raise the price of jute, and make it more profitable to the cultivator to grow jute than paddy, he will naturally resume jute cultivation to the prejudice of paddy cultivation. This follows a universal economic law. And any interference with it will not only deprive the producer of his legitimate economic freedom but will inevitably inflict an obvious injury on the entire economy of his life.

Indeed, it is difficult to understand why, if Europe is really threatened with what the "*Times*" apprehends, "a world scarcity of food" there should be any necessity to "*force* Asia to wear old clothes in order that Europe may not starve." A world-famine like this, following the present dreadful war, which has already dislocated every European industry which is not essential to war-work, will be bound to prejudicially affect the exportation of raw materials from India. This apprehended famine will be bound to interfere with European industries and lead to a consequent fall in the demand for raw materials from India. The economic incentive to produce industrial crops, at the cost of food grains, will be gone. The cultivator will be forced, by normal economic reasons, to turn his attention to increase the production of the food grains, which will pay him more, from the production of industrial crops which will inevitably pay less. To the uninitiated, there seems to exist, therefore, absolutely no reason to call for state-interference with the agricultural life and labour of the people of India and "force them to wear old clothes in order that Europe may not starve."

The "*Times*" foresees all this, and, therefore, offers "a word of warning by way of conclusion." If the War Cabinet should unhappily be driven to the decision, (it says) "that India's peasants must be mobilised in the interests of the world's food, the operation must be so conducted as to afford no scope for a cry of exploitation."

> "The peasant will be asked to sacrifice his independence; that sacrifice ought to suffice, and he should not be required to undertake increased financial liabilities. In other words, the curtailment of industrial crops

> must be accompanied by a guarantee of minimum prices for food grains, sufficient to ensure that the peasant should not be a loser."

I fail to see why the peasant should be a loser by producing food grains instead of industrial crops, unless the price of these latter in the open market of the world be higher than that of food grains. And if the normal price of food grains be lower than that of industrial crops, in other words, if the value of food grains produced upon an acre be less than the value of any industrial crops that may be raised on the same area, the minimum prices of food grains that will be "sufficient to ensure that the peasant shall not be a loser" must be equivalent to what he might receive from his industrial crops.

And the question is—Will the food grains sell cheaper or dearer than industrial crops in the world's market? If they sell dearer, there is no need of any state-interference or guarantee. If they sell cheaper, then the minimum price to be guaranteed must be more than the normal market value of the produce. And who will pay the difference between what the peasant might have received from the open market for his industrial crops and what he will receive from the food grains that he may be "forced" by the Government to produce? The guarantee of the State can only be met out of public revenues. In other words, the Indian nation will have to pay to the peasant for the supply of cheap food to Europe. I am afraid, however, that the economics of the "*Times*" did not consider all these things, when it talked of guaranteeing minimum prices for food grains. Its idea evidently was to fix this minimum not in the terms of the profit which the peasant might get if he had produced industrial crops instead of food grains, but only in relation to the prices of food grains in the world market.

The full significance of this "humanitarian" scheme lies in the preparation which it will make for the "mobilisation" of the entire economic resources of the country, so that what the "*Times*" calls the "self-governing Empire" may "develop" the natural resources of India in the interests of British and Colonial industry. This experiment "upon an otherwise impossible scale" in controlling the agricultural resources of the country, and "the conversion of private into quasi-public business" (as the "ELEMENTS OF RECONSTRUCTION" put it in (another context), will make the way clear for the working out of the proposed economic policy of "profit-sharing state-partnership with private capitalist amalgamations."

For, though the machinery of land administration in India may be successfully employed to control agricultural production, there is no Government agency that exists at present or may be created in the future, which will be able to handle the increased food-production contemplated in the *Times'* scheme. Existing exporting houses will have to be necessarily used for this purpose. And they will have to be given monopoly-rights—called "licenses" in civilised parlance—in this business. The control of food-products, both in the matter of production and in that of the export of these products, will be helpful to the carrying out of the new economic policy. The experience thus gained will be of great value in the control of industrial crops also, and the machinery thus created would be ready to be used for the production and distribution of these products as well.

XXI

AMERICAN AND JAPANESE INVASION OF THE INDIAN MARKET

AND the need for it is not less, but, perhaps even more, than that of simply feeding Europe; because, without some such control, it will be—we do not say impossible—but exceedingly difficult for Great Britain to overtake her friendly rivals, America and Japan, in the race for industrial advance and the capture of world-markets. These four and half years of war have completely disorganised British industry. Both men and machinery had to be drafted for war-work. But, while British plants and works were turning out explosives, and British workingmen were engaged either in fighting the enemy at different fronts or making shells and other war-necessaries, Japanese and American plants and works were turning out enormous quantities of commodities for the use of the civil populations of the world, and quietly, but therefore none-the-less effectively, taking possession of the markets that had hitherto been under the exclusive possession of the British.

A mere glance at the statistics of our export and import trade for the years from 1909–'10 to 1917–'18 shows that both America and Japan, specially the latter, have very considerably captured the trade of India.

AVERAGE OF OUR IMPORT TRADE

	PRE-WAR (1909-'10 TO '13-'14,)	1917-'18
Great Britain.........	63 per cent.	54 per cent.
Other parts of the British Empire	7 "	10 "
Other foreign countries except Allies and Java	13 "	4 "

Java ...	6 per cent.	8 per cent.
Allies (other than Japan and United States A).	6 "	4 "
America ...	3 "	8 "
Japan ...	2 "	12 "
	Total—100.	Total—100.

The following are the figures for our Export Trade :

	Pre-War 1909-'10 to '13-'14	1917-'18.
United Kingdom	25 per cent	26 per cent.
Other parts of the British Empire	17 "	27 "
Other Foreign Countries (except Allies)	23 "	10 "
Allies other than Japan and United States	21 "	10 "
United States	7 "	13 "
Japan	7 "	14 "
	Total—100.	Total—100.

" The most interesting fact that emerges from an examination of these figures (to quote the " Review of the Trade of India" —1917-'18), is the large increase in our trade with Japan and the United States. The total trade with Japan in 1917-'18 exceeded that with any other country except the United Kingdom. Japan now holds the second place in India's import and export trade. Mr. O'Connor, late Director-General of Statistics, in his Review of the Trade of India for the year ending 31st March 1889, wrote " Imports from Japan are quite trifling, averaging less than three lakhs annually in the last five years, and there are no indications of an increase unless the imports of copper should be resumed." When the long list of imports at the present time is examined, the progress in our trade with Japan cannot be termed other than phenomenal. The value of the imports from Japan in 1917-'18 was 400 per cent. above the pre-war quenquennial average, while the exports increased by 103 per cent."

As regards the trade with the United States, in the year 1917-'18, it was (to quote from the "Review" again) "double that in the pre-war period and second only to that of Japan. The total value amounted to Rs 42 crores, almost the same as in the preceding year, of which imports were Rs. 12 crores and exports Rs. 30 crores. As compared with the pre-war quenquennium, imports increased by 163 per cent. and exports by 81 per cent."

All these offer very great food for serious thought to the Indian publicists and politicians, in the benevolent scheme suggested by the *Times* for doubling or even trebling the surplus food which India sends to Europe "at the cost of curtailing the supply of raw materials and of forcing Asia to wear old clothes," (instead of new ones imported from Japan or America) "in order that Europe may not starve."

XXII

HONORARY WAR-WORK AND ECONOMIC EXPLOITATION

As in the United Kingdom so also in India organisations for war-work have been of very material help in preparing the ground for the new economic reconstruction. In India the Munition Boards have already taken a full survey of India's natural resources required for munition-making. These resources have, besides military, also very supreme economic value. The information collected and the experience gained by the Munition Boards will be at the disposal of capitalists and commercial men. True it is that Indian capitalists and commercial men will have equal access to these informations as their British rivals. But, as Sir Sankaran Nair points out in his Note of Dissent, "we know that it is the commercial organisations in England that would be able to utilise it."

And already there are evidences in all directions of the initiation of new commercial enterprises by British capitalists in every Indian province since the cessation of hostilities, and most energetic efforts have commenced to be put forth by British capital with a view to capture Indian trades and industries. There is, in the surface-view of it, nothing wrong in all this. As Lord Curzon pointed out many years ago, "Capital is international." Wherever capital finds prospects of profit and assurance of peaceful penetration, it flows there by its own inner stimulus. India offers this favourable field; and we cannot blame British capitalists if they are ever ready to take advantage of the economic dis-organisation of our country and reap whatever benefit they can get out of it. In fact, to quote Sir Sankaran Nair again, "we know that we cannot do without English capital." But we are not able to obtain it on the same terms generally on which it would be lent to the Colonies and other countries. "The terms must be those agreed upon between the English capitalists and competent Indians who will protect Indian interests." But, unfortunately,

> "The English officials in India and the Indian Office have not in the past protected India. They have submitted to English capitalists, and I have no doubt will do so in future. We want Englishmen to start industries in India, but not to the detriment of indigenous industries. It is quite clear to me that unless there is an Indian to protect Indian industries, we will have English firms starting industries on a large scale in India (in which Indians will have very little share), to the detriment of Indian industries."

The Munitions Board has opened up new and more effective avenues of exploitation of our natural resources by foreign, and particularly British capitalists. The heads of some of the most enterprising mercantile houses in India were drafted into this Board as honorary officers. Without their help the Munitions Board could not possibly work efficiently. The same thing had been done in England also. These gentlemen had gained in the course of their work in connection with the Munitions Board exceedingly valuable information which it is only natural that they should now use for their own business or trade.

The same thing is happening in England also. Civil servants, employed under the Munitions Board, are being tempted to resign their position to take up employment in private commercial enterprises. A London weekly paper recently noticed this:

"Quite a number of highly-placed Civil servants

are resigning their position to take up more remunerative employment in private enterprise and the fact is exciting a certain amount of uneasiness in commercial circles. It is natural enough that men of energy and ambition should welcome the chance of escaping from the deadly routine of Government service : but the motives of those who have offered them engagements are a little suspect. In their official position these ex-Civil servants have had access to returns and information supplied to the Government in confidence by firms all over the country, and it is obvious that this knowledge would be of the greatest value to trade rivals. Even with the most honourable intentions, a man thus informed, would inevitably determine his action by his special cognisance, and hence the uneasiness with which these appointments are regarded."

This experience is also being repeated in India. We too have had one or two instances of members of the Civil Service resigning their position to take up more remunerative employment in new commercial enterprises. If I remember aright, one of these gentlemen who was connected with the Munitions Board has been taken up by the Tatas. Messrs. Mackintosh Burn & Co. of Calcutta are also reported to have engaged a high-placed gentleman lately employed under the Munitions Board, to help them in their new concrete ship-building and kindred activities. All these are indications of increased and more energetic efforts for the exploitation of our natural resources and abundant cheap labour "by private capitalist amalgamations."

XXIII

INDIAN PARTICIPATION IN THE COMPANY "BOOM"

THE prospect of after-war-trade and the natural desire of Indian capitalists to reap their share of these, have also led to the organisation of a few Indian Companies for the utilisation of our immense natural resources. These good people seem to think that this is the only practical way by which foreign capitalist exploitation of our economic life and capabilities, may, to some extent at least, be checked. But the work is absolutely hopeless. In the first place, we have not the quantity of fluid capital in the country which could enter into effective competition with foreign capitalist exploitation. In the next place, Indian enterprises of this kind which require machineries and accessories for the work, are inevitably dependent upon foreign manufacturers and shipping concerns for the supply of these. The whole Indian trade of Great Britain or America, for instance, in these machineries is in the hands of foreigners. They are the exporters of these here. If we try to get behind them and deal directly with the manufacturers, even there we shall find that there are the inevitable middlemen, except through whom no British or American manufacturer, does any business directly with the customers. There are wheels within wheels and subtle tricks of trade which render it practically impossible for Indian importers to deal directly and profitably with foreign exporters and manufacturers. We may deal directly, if we are so anxious to do it; but we shall have to pay "catalogue prices," which are rarely or never the real prices of things. Those who have any experiences of "direct" dealings with foreign manufacturers and have had any inside knowledge of how things are done, in these foreign countries, know that to try to override foreign agencies in these matters is to court, not gain, but loss. If India had large manufacturing concerns and if there was anything like the spirit of combination among them, which operates in British industries, then possibly thev could force the hands of foreign machine-makers and introduce Indian agencies in this trade. But we are just starting these concerns. We are without expert knowledge and large experience of the working of these large enterprises. Our capitalists with just one or two solitary exceptions, like those of the Tatas, for instance, are consequently at the complete mercy of the foreigner. It is no wonder, therefore, that these enterprises so often come to grief. The idea, therefore, of successfully or appreciably stemming the inroads of British capitalism into India, by the organisation of Indian capital, is simply preposterous.

Profitable foreign trade-connections are impossible without foreign agencies. Whether we are buyers or we are sellers, we must have these agencies, if our trade is to be retained in our own hands. But there are few Indian agencies in England or America. The Tatás have a London office, who represent them to British manufacturers, and this is we think about the only Indian agency worth mentioning in the United Kingdom. And even the Tatas found it no easy job to establish themselves in London. Indian enterprises which do not command the huge financial resources of the Tatas cannot expect to establish themselves in the same way or to the same extent as the Tatas have done. Indian capitalist enterprise, entering into any present or prospective competitions with British capital, whether here or in England, have to face endless difficulties. In the first place, there is the differential treatment which they receive here from individual official. This is very keenly felt in regard to the acquisition of land for big agricultural or manufacturing concerns. The land laws and the Board of Revenue regulations affecting the transfer of rights all work, in practice, to the prejudice of Indian enterprise. Foreign firms, owing to the intimate social relations of their representatives with the foreign officials in the country, are able to secure lands for their works far more easily than Indian concerns. This has been an almost common grievance in the Bengal districts, for instance, the soil of which is favourable for Tea-cultivation. I do not know if it is so in the other provinces also. But the Industrial Commission has, as I have pointed out already, noticed the difficulties of land-acquisition, and has proposed certain alterations in the existing laws on the subject, which are calculated to remove these difficulties. These changes or improvements will, no doubt, be made for the benefit of Indian industrial enterprise generally, without any discrimination as to the race or colour of the capitalists interested in these enterprises. They are all equal before the law. This has always been the legitimate pride of the British Government in India. But in practice, owing to inevitable social influences, these advantages will work more readily and in an immensely larger measure, for foreign than for indigenous enterprises. In the next place, there are difficulties, as already indicated, in the way of forming foreign connections upon the same terms as our rivals in business. Thirdly, there are banking difficulties, owing to the absence of large and prosperous Indian banking houses both in this and in foreign countries, capable of commanding the influence of both indigenous and foreign trade. Fourthly, there is a lack of large business experience and proficiency. Fifthly, there is a total absence of what may be called the very essence of success in all corporate and co-operative enterprises, namely, the habit of mind which subordinates all personal vanities and private parsimoniousness or greed to the one supreme desire to help the success of the common enterprise. In the face of these difficulties and disabilities, it is unreasonable to hope that we shall be able to successfully compete with foreign capitalist enterprises, in the development of our natural resources. And when one thinks of all these difficulties, one finds the economic situation in the country almost hopeless.

XXIV

ORGANIC RELATION BETWEEN INDUSTRIALISM AND IMPERIALISM

THIS economic situation may be summed up by one simple phrase, namely, extensive exploitation of our natural resources, our cheap labour and our large markets by British capital in alliance with the political authority of the Imperial and the Indian Governments. What has been done on a comparatively small scale during the last hundred years and more will now be attempted upon a huge scale. This necessity has been forced upon Imperial politicians by the financial and economic condition brought about by the recent war. The British Chancellor of the Exchequer will have to find additional revenues to the tune of between seven and eight hundred millions a year to meet war-obligations. It is admitted that it is impossible to raise this amount by fresh taxation. The only means suggested for it is the exploitation of the natural resources of the Empire by the State in partnership with capitalist amalgamations. This new economic policy has also been forced upon British politicians by the internal condition of their own country. The long-drawn conflict between labour and capital cannot safely be permitted to continue any further. The continuance of this conflict under the new psychological and social conditions created by the war would lead to the breakup of the whole political and economic structure of the Empire. Means must be found, therefore, to settle this conflict as quickly and as effectively as possible. In the settlement of this conflict labour will have to be paid a much larger share of the profits of the industries which they had helped to make, than before. This can only be done by increasing the profits of capital. These profits can no longer be earned only by the employment of capital in "home" industries. These latter have almost reached their limit. Consequently, capitalists who are masters of works in the United Kingdom must be induced to extend their operations to the other parts of the Empire, particularly to the Dependencies where there is an abundant supply of raw material and an unlimited amount of cheap labour. If these materials can be worked into commodities on the spot where they are produced or found, it will contribute materially to the reduction of the cost of these productions. And if cheap labour is employed in these works, the cost of production will be further reduced. All this will tend to increase the profits of the capitalist classes, and enable them without any sacrifice to meet new and increased demands made for higher wages by "home" labour upon their resources. This is the whole situation. And it offers a very grave menace to our economic future and freedom.

This danger cannot be averted by any effort that we may possibly put forth to organise indigenous capital and compete with foreign capitalist enterprises in our home industry. We have, for one thing, neither sufficient capital nor sufficient enterprise for this purpose. In the next place, the machinery of the State among us is not under our control, but is largely controlled, both in England and in India, by British and Anglo-Indian capitalists. But even if we had the capital, enterprise and control over our state machinery, it would be ruinous to our national life in almost every aspect of it if we tried to imitate or emulate British or European industrialism. In the first place, we must never forget that this industrialism is organically bound up with European Imperialism. The two cannot be separated one from the other. This industrialism means quick and enormous production of commodities. But commodities are useless without adequate markets for their disposal. All the British works would collapse in a day if the commodities they produce did not find ready and increasing market in the various Dependencies of the Empire. These Dependencies must be maintained in the interest of British industrialism itself. We have no dependencies. We cannot dump foreign markets with our excess produce. Consequently, in the absence of a dependent Empire, governed and controlled by us, the development of our industry along European lines and upon the large scale in which these industries have been built in the western countries would be suicidal folly on our part. All these things should be carefully considered by those who fancy that the economic regeneration of India will come from the introduction of European industrialism into this country.

XXV

DANGERS OF IMITATING EUROPEAN INDUSTRIALISM IN INDIA

THERE are graver and more vital issues involved in this rage for European industrialism among us. Our greatest problem is how to relieve the pressure on land which has resulted from the decadence and destruction of our ancient manufacturers. More than 88% of our populations live on agriculture. And as our agricultural operations depend entirely upon favourable monsoons and adequate rainfall, the least disturbance of these conditions develop sudden failure of these operations, throwing large masses of people on to the very brink of starvation. The only remedy for our chronic distress and poverty is to relieve this excessive pressure on our agricultural works. This is the supreme and vital need for developing manufacturing industries in this country. And the question is, will the introduction of modern European industrialism help or hinder the solution of this problem? In other words, will this relieve the pressure on land of our teeming populations?

Modern European industrialism means, among other things, the employment of machineries for the production of commodities. Machineries are useful in two ways: first, they help to save labour, and, secondly, help quick production. In its labour-saving aspect, the introduction of machineries inevitably lead to increased un-employment of the labouring populations. Where, for instance, to produce a certain quantity of commodities, it would require the labour of twenty men, with the help of machineries it can be produced by ten men. The result, therefore, is that the employment of machinery throws ten men in every twenty out of employ. It means, in plain English, that what are called labour-saving appliances for the production of commodities, really result in labourer-starving also. This is why unemployment has grown frightfully in England with the growth of these machine-made industries. Our central problem being to find employment for our populations, now dependent upon agriculture, in new works and factories, the pursuit of European methods for the revival of our manufactures, will not at all solve this problem; but will only help to increase its gravity and complexity.

Nor should we forget that the essential character of our socio-economic structure was its freedom from what is known as capitalism in modern Europe. Our artisans and manufacturers were never exclusively artisans or manufacturers, except in the great cities. All over the country they joined their crafts and arts to their essential agricultural occupations. Expert artists and craftsmen enjoyed freehold land from which they got their subsistence. Consequently, they did not need outside capital to keep their families going, during the time they were engaged in the production of their wares and until these were ready for the market. The economic independence of our artisans and craftsmen was thus fully secured in the past. Our skilled labourers, who produced all our old manufacturers, were thus hardly labourers in the European sense of the term. They were both masters and workmen combined in one. They worked together upon the principle of co-operative labour, and on communistic basis; each family joining together and pooling both their labour and their material for the production of works of art, or other manufactures, which remained the property of all the members of the family, and there was no one to claim, as capitalist, the lion's share of the profits of their produce. And we must very seriously think it over whether the pursuit of modern European methods of industrial development will be conducive to our social well-being and moral uplift, or, whether by so doing we shall only be importing the problems of European industrialism, mistaking these as perfect solutions of the problem before us.

The most obvious thing in this European industrialism is that it has all through been seeking to produce commodity at the cost of the humanity of the labouring populations. No one can pass through any of the great industrial centres in the United Kingdom or even in America, without being sickeningly impressed with the ruin of human body, mind, and soul that results from modern industrial methods. Europe has, however, been gradually finding a remedy against these evils in the expansion of democratic franchise. The labourers in almost every European country have acquired political power. They have been given the vote; and they have been using it increasingly for the protection of their own interests and the organisation of their own forces with a view to successfully fight capitalism. Trade Unionism, Syndicalism, Socialism, and various other "isms" owe their birth to the vote of labour in all the democratic countries of the west. The fight between labour and capital is, therefore, not so unequal as it was at one time. The might of labour is daily growing; and in this, labour has a compensation for the inevitable wrongs which it has had to suffer at the hand of capital. But the contest is far from being over or even nearing its end. Where this fight will lead to, no one can foretell with any degree of confidence. It may be possible to work up some sort of an abiding reconciliation between the interests of labour and those of capital. Or, failing this, this fight may ultimately end in the general break-up of modern European industrialism and economic structure. No one can say what will come to pass. Every thing is just now in a flux. And, in view of it all, Indian statesmanship cannot rashly run after this European industrialism as a panacea for our economic evils and a solution for our very vital economic problems.

So far as can be seen, our future lies not in the mad attempt to imitate or emulate modern European industrialism, but rather in putting up a tough fight against it. It will no doubt be an unequal and almost impossible fight, we know. The forces of this industrialism have at their back all the authority of both the Indian and the Imperial Government. They are also supported by the natural greed of our own new-born capitalist classes. There are also others, who are neither capitalists nor Government men, but who have been so completely obsessed with this modern industrialism, that they too will, and indeed, are already lending their intellectual and moral support to this new spirit of imitative economic reform and progress. All these cannot be denied, and ought not to be ignored. All these make the work of real and constructive economic reforms exceedingly difficult for us.

XXVI

THE RESUME

THE financial and economic situation before Imperial statesmen just now is marked by:

1. A depleted Exchequer, which is being saved from open bankruptcy by a reckless and an almost unlimited creation of paper money without any decent treasury reserve at its back;
2. Overwhelming financial obligations imposed by the last war, which with the continuation of military or quasi-military operations in Russia and elsewhere, involve, on the most moderate computation, a total daily expenditure of 4 million pounds, or about 1,450 million pounds a year, as estimated by the *Times* and the *Daily News* in September last;

3. The impossibility, (as admitted in Parliament, by Mr. Amery at the beginning of 1919, in course of the debate over the address to the King), of meeting these new obligations out of the normal revenues of the country;

4. The enunciation by responsible Imperial financeers and politicians of a new economic policy, having for its objective the development of the resources of the Empire under some sort of a scheme of profit-sharing co-partnership between the State and private capitalist amalgamations or corporations;

5. The abandonment of the old economic dogma of Free Trade in favour of Imperial Preference;

6. The accumulation of huge profits made during the war through war work in the hands of a small body of capitalists;

7. The disorganised condition of British industries due to the war;

8. The serious unrest among the British working classes who demand not only a share in the profits of the works in which they are engaged but also a substantial share in the management of these works; and
9. The new menace to capitalist exploitation in the United Kingdom which the new Labour movement has openly created.

All these have combined to force British capital out of the United Kingdom to the Colonies, Dependencies and Protectorates of the Empire. A very vigorous attempt will be presently made to exploit our immense raw material and our cheap labour in the interests of British capitalism; and, as this exploitation will be either directly or indirectly protected by the authority of the Government of India and helped by the organisations already at the command of this Government, it constitutes a very serious economic and political menace to us.

In fact, it is difficult to resist the conviction that the real inwardness of the new policy inaugurated by the announcement of August 20, 1917, and materialised in recent legislations both in India and in England, dealing with the present Indian situation, can only be discovered in the new economic motive of the present capitalist government. Ever since the announcement of August 20, 1917, the authorities have been anxious to stop all agitation for political rights in India.

Few people seem to recognise the organic relation that exists between the Rowlat Act and present Reform Act. It is notorious that the real motive of the announcement of August 20, 1917 was, as Lord Islington, the then Under-Secretary of State for India frankly admitted in the House of Lords, to relieve "the gravity" of the Indian situation, which meant, in other words, to allay the unrest created by our agitation for the early establishment of complete self-government in India. Para 150 of the Montagu-Chelmsford's Report made this object absolutely clear. Here we had the clearest possible indication that the passage of the proposed reforms would either be preceded or accompanied by the arming of the Government with such powers of the law as will be sufficient for the maintenance of order. The authors of this Joint-Report said:

> "Now that His Majesty's Government have declared their policy, reasonable men have something which they can oppose successfully to the excitement created by attacks on government and by abuse of Englishmen, coupled with glowing and inaccurate accounts of India's golden past and appeals to race hatred in the name of religion. Many prominent Indians dislike and fear such methods. A new opportunity is now being offered to combat them; and we expect them to take it. Disorder must be prejudicial

to the cause of progress, and specially disorder as a political weapon. But we have no hesitation in recommending that the government must maintain power to prevent the disastrous consequences, if in any case law and order are jeopardised."

Here we have the whole policy of the reforms laid bare. Mr. Montagu has been anxious that henceforth Indian publicists and politicians should whole-heartedly apply themselves to work out his reforms and not lend themselves to any outside agitation for forcing the pace of progress. Lord Sinha has been repeating the same thing. In his address to his "moderate" friends in Bombay his lordship said: "I say with all humility that the pace would be accelerated not by what we call agitation but by real, solid, substantial results"; and that "the new constitution that we have got, if worked properly, will lead us to responsible government to the same extent as is now enjoyed by the self-governing countries of His Majesty's dominions." All this is merely a repetition of the advice offered by the joint-Report.

It is also significant that the whole body of the capitalist press in England with the *Times* at their head had been persistently urging the passage of the Reform Act with as little delay as possible, which could only be prompted by a desire to draw a red herring across our path and divert attention from the more vital processes of economic exploitation upon the success of which will very largely if not entirely depend the future of Imperialist-capitalist interests.

This is the great economic menace with which we stand face to face. It consists in the increased, organised, and most likely state-aided attempt of British capital to exploit our natural resources and our cheap labour. And the question is—

WHAT IS THE REMEDY?

We are helpless. The power of the State is not in our hands. We cannot control our tariff; we cannot make a levy upon capital; we cannot legislate about the acquisition of land or mining rights by foreign capitalists; we cannot even pass any labour legislation. All these are in the hands of the representatives of this very capitalist class. The British Parliament, democratic in name, is really capitalist in character. The British Cabinet, nominally responsible to the British democracy, is really the slave and servant of the plutocracy. The Government in India is subject to the control of this British Cabinet and British Parliament. It is notoriously dominated by the influence of the Chambers of Commerce in India, representing British capitalist enterprise in this country. What can we do then? Ancient Hindu Polity says: When you are face to face with a powerful enemy, your only way of safety lies in an alliance with an equally powerful friend who is opposed to your enemy.

XXVII

ALLIANCE WITH BRITISH LABOUR PARTY

BRITISH labour-socialist party is this friend. And our only hope of safety lies in an open alliance with this political party in the United Kingdom. At one time, we sought to ally ourselves with the British Liberals, but we gradually discovered that Liberals or Tories made really little or no difference so far as the real interests of India were concerned. We now know that Liberals or Tories, they are all plutocrats. They all belong to the capitalist, exploiting and profiteering classes. And in our fight with British capitalism, we have absolutely no hope of help either from the Liberal or Tory politicians in England. Frankly speaking, British Liberalism is dying, if it is not already dead; no longer a power in British politics. There are at present only two dominant political forces in the United Kingdom and the Empire : the force of capital and the force of labour. These two are coming into a fatal grip with one another. Therefore our only chance of safety in our present condition of political impotence and economic helplessness lies in an open, courageous, and uncompromising alliance with British Labour.

XXVIII

COMMUNITY OF SELF-INTEREST

AND this alliance is possible because of the community of interest between us and British Labour. British Labour is slowly coming to realise the very serious menace which the increased exploitation of our raw materials and cheap labour by British capital has commenced to offer to British Labour interests. Capitalism, if it becomes powerful in the Empire will be bound to re-act upon labour-conditions in the United Kingdom. British capitalists have already commenced to hold up the bogey of Indian competition to frighten British Labour into a reasonable attitude. The fact of the matter, however, is that this so-called

Indian competition does not signify competition with strangers at all but practically with the same capitalist who are exploiting Indian resources and Indian Labour with raw materials near at hand and with the frugal Labour of India which could be easily exploited without any trouble, because the Indian Labourers do not possess the inconvenient rights and privileges of the British working men, British capitalist enterprise in India, directly or indirectly supported by the Government of India offer really a very serious menace to the economic interests of the British working classes. India's political freedom, built upon a wide democratic basis, which would give the Indian workers, whether mental or manual or industrial or agricultural, the same right to control the Indian Executive as are now enjoyed by the British working classes, would offer the only protection to the British working classes against Indian competition. Those who are engaged in the fight for freedom in India are really struggling for rights which, once secured by the Indian people, will be bound to benefit the British working classes, though it will hurt British capitalist interests in India. Here, then, is an appeal to the enlightened self-interest of the British workers which will help to build up an alliance between Indian Nationalism and British Labour.

But British Labour will not touch us even with a pair of tongs unless we are prepared to fight indigenous capitalism in India, even as we are prepared to fight imported British capitalism.

The new economic menace, as we have already seen, comes through two things, first, our immense, and, second, our cheap labour. These are the two things that tempt British capital into India. We cannot destroy our raw materials, and remove the first cause of this temptation. But we can very largely, if not wholly, remove the second temptation. We can

XXIX

ORGANISE INDIAN LABOUR

SO that it will henceforth refuse to work for the present scale of wages, and accept the present hours of work. Indian Labour must be organised to put up a demand for relatively equal wages and absolutely the same hours as British Labour. Our Labourers must have the same wages as British Labourers relatively to the cost of living in India. Indian working men, whether in our railways or in our mines, or in any other works, must have the same wages that are paid to the European or Eurasian employees engaged in the same work. At present they receive lower wages than the European or Eurasian workers. This differential wage-system must at once be abolished. The same work must receive the same wages, whatever may be the colour of the workman. In other departments Indian workers, whether engaged in manual or mental work, must be paid wages that shall bear the same relation to the cost of living in India as the wages of the similar class of Labour in England bear to the general cost of living there. The Indian workers in every field of our social and economic life must demand and receive wages not only enough to keep body and soul together but wages sufficient to enable them and those dependent on them to cultivate and improve their fullest manhood.

This must be our first demand.

Our next demand must be for an absolute equalisation of the hours of work between Indian and British Labour. The American Labour Congress have already formulated a demand for a maximum of forty-eight hours a week. India must also enter into the same compact. This maximum of forty-eight hours a week for Labour in India must be definitely fixed by legislation. The proportional and relative equalisation of wages and the absolute equalisation of the hours of work of Indian Labour with British and European Labour generally remove that cheapness of Indian Labour which offers now so strong a temptation to foreign capital to come and exploit it. This will to a very large extent remove all unfair competition between capitalist enterprise in India and the United Kingdom and the Colonies. It will bring the Labour-Socialist forces in the United Kingdom, and indeed, all over the modern world into friendly alliance with the Nationalist-Democratic movement in India.

But even this increased wages of Labour and equal hours of work with United Kingdom in India, will still leave a large margin of profits to capitalist exploitation in this country, owing to the presence of our immense raw materials, and leave enough room for unfair competition between India and the outside world. With a view to bring working class interests in India into line with those of the United Kingdom and the Colonies, we shall have to do something more.

XXX

ALL EXCESS-PROFITS MUST BE TAXED

THERE is no reason why capitalist exploiters in India should appropriate 150, 250 or, 350, and in some cases even 400 per cent. divident on their capital outlay; and why, whatever earnings may be made in any business should not, beyond a certain reasonable percentage, come to the State. If we can compel all these Excess-Profits to flow into the Public Exchequer, we shall have enough money to pay for everything that we want, enough money to improve sanitation, enough money to spend on the education of our people, enough money to help them to grow to the fullest stature of their manhood.

If we can put up a fight for these things, namely, increased wages and shorter hours for our Labourers, and the expropriation of all Excess-Profits by the State to be spent upon measures needed for the health, happiness and the intellectual and moral uplift of the Indian masses, we have not the least shadow or suspicion of a doubt that we can immediately form a close, intimate, and helpful alliance with British, nay world Labour. And we shall be able to use this alliance not only for our economic protection and salvation, but also for the political emancipation of our people.

XXXI

CONDITIONS OF THE PROBLEM

A STUDY of the present Indian and world-situation demands this new Nationalist policy. This alliance with British Labour and the equalisation of wages and hours of work in India with those in Great Britain and other Western countries will have a far-reaching effect upon present international relations, and will help very materially to remove the most powerful cause of the present racial conflict. In fact, this will help more than anything else to solve a most touchy and difficult Imperial problem, the problem, namely, of India's relations with British over-seas Dominions. We have been used hitherto to look upon the opposition of these Dominions to receive Indian immigrants into their territories upon equal terms with European emigrants as an insult to our colour and culture. There may be some element of colour-conceit and culture-pride at the back of it. But the real reason is economic. The Indian Labourers receive lower wages than European working men, and these lower wages, while contributing to the increased profits of the capitalist exploiters indirectly hurts the vital economic interests of their White Labour. The demand for the equalisation of wages with those of European workers by Indian Labour, whether in India itself or in the Colonies, will at once help to remove the present sense of economic wrong which India's cheap Labour inflicts directly or indirectly upon British and European Labour employed in the Colonies. It is a mistake to view the present struggle in South Africa between our emigrants and the Boer settlers as a purely racial problem. The systematic crusade against Asiatic emigration into Canada and the United States as well into Australia and New Zealand is also largely, if not entirely, due to this economic cause. And this cause can only be removed by the adoption of this new policy.

We know that there will be a strong opposition to this policy from the capitalist interests in the country. Capitalists have always opposed factory legislation calculated to improve labour conditions affecting their profits. Increase of wages and shortening of hours of work are not therefore likely to be viewed with favour by our own actual or prospective capitalists and owners of industries. They will plead the existing difficulties in their way and the impossibility of competing with European industries or with the new and growing industries of American and Japan for opposing this new Labour policy in India. There are others among us who though not directly interested in capitalist exploitation have a sort of an idea that India's economic advancement and salvation must come from the development of modern industrialism in the country and the equipment of the Indian nation for successful competition with European, American or Japanese industries. They do not seem to clearly realise either the actualities of industrial conditions in India or in the outside world. They are anxious to equip themselves with every modern appliance for the production of cheap commodities in large quantities, without which they believe, it will not be possible for them to successfully compete with their rivals. But they ignore one fundamental fact in connection with the development of modern European industrialism.

This fact, as has been already noted in

these pages, is the intimate and organic relation between Imperialism and modern industrialism. Quick and enormous production of Commodities is profitable only when the producer can command extensive markets for the disposal of his commodities. In other words, helpless and unprotected markets under the control of the producer are an essential condition of the success of modern industrialism. Great Britain led this industrialism because she had acquired an extensive Empire on which she could dump her goods. Political Imperialism is organically bound up with modern industrialism. Industrialism and Imperialism are joined like the proverbial Siamese twins. They can never be separated and live. Those who among us are obsessed with the fancy that by simply adopting European appliances and method and utilising our immense raw materials and cheap labour, they will be able to produce commodities cheap in price and sufficiently large in quantity to successfully compete with similar commodities produced in England, forget that the moment they threaten British capitalist interests, means will be found by the Government both here and in England which are practically controlled by these powerful interests to check the success of Industrialism in India. The imposition of the excise duty on Indian cotton goods proves the reality of this danger. As long as India has not attained complete fiscal autonomy and the representatives of national interests have not secured full control of the national state, so long even Indian capitalist interest have not the ghost of a chance of protecting themselves against hurtful competition from British capitalist interests.

There is yet another reason why we must try, so far as may be, to stop this fatal inroad. Every British sovereign invested by British capitalists in Indian industrial enterprise means not only so much economic power and the control of our economic life by the foreign exploiter, but, what is far more dangerous, also a corresponding volume of political power. Already the Government of India is almost overwhelmingly controlled by British capitalist interests in the country. The increase of British capital in India will inevitably lead to increased control of the Government by the representatives of British capital. These have always been more or less openly opposed to the expansion of political freedom in the country. The most relentless opposition even to the very insignificant advance sought to be secured by Mr. Montagu's Reform Act has come from this class. And this capitalist will always do the same. They obstruct the course of constitutional advance of the

Indian people and the democratisation of the Government in India. For political, as much as for economic reasons, we must therefore adopt timely measures to prevent any new accession of power to British capitalist interest in this country.

XXXII

IN DEFENCE OF OUR CULTURE

THERE is, thirdly, yet another reason for the adoption of this new Labour policy. It is the only policy that can possibly prevent any further development of capitalist industrial enterprises among us. Few people seem to realise how the advance of the modern industrial spirit resulting from our economic and political relations with Great Britain has already commenced to break up our old economic and social structure, and revolutionise all the ancient ethical and spiritual values of life. No social reformer, however aggressive or radical, has been able or could ever expect to break up our society in the way and to the extent that this modern industrialism has already and is increasingly doing. It has set up in place of our old caste system, based on birth and heredity, a new order of social precedence and honour based on wealth. Our old castes, in spite of all their limitations, were within caste limits, essentially democratic institutions. Within the caste honour and precedence went always by age and character, but rarely or never by wealth or material prosperity. Among the so-called "depressed" classes, it was always so. But the advance of modern capitalist industrialism is killing this spirit of independence and democracy in every caste and community. A man's worth has already commenced to be measured not by a man's intellectual endowments or spiritual acquisition but by the length of his purse and the extent of his possessions. Character counts for much less to-day in the scale of social values among us than learning or morals. It never was so. Our aristocracy was an aristocracy of intellect and character. The Brahmins were, as a class, the poorest in the community. The ideal may have been mediæval; but it saved us in any case from the corroding evils of the wealth-dominated class-system of modern Europe. If we desire to preserve what was morally and spiritually the best in our culture and character, we must immediately put up a strong fight against the inroads of modern capitalist industrialism. And in this fight our only possible allies are British and European Labour.

Lastly, we desire the adoption of this new policy not merely for economic or political reasons, but from the highest religious and spiritual motive also. To us every being represents the potential Divine. The development of God-in-Man, to bring out the latent Divinity in every human being, is the ideal-end of all social endeavour and national evolution. Every Brahmin cites in his daily devotions the couplet which says—

> I am God, none other; I am Brahman and not subject to grief or bereavement; I am of the nature of the True, the Illumined and the Blessed. I am eternally Free.

This sums up the ideal-end of all individual or social endeavour in our thought and culture. The object of the social life and social disciplines is to bring out this Divine nature in every man and woman. The ignorance of man prevents the revolution of the light of God in him. The degradation of man degrades the Deity who resides in him. The bondage of man hurts the freedom of God. This is our philosophy of life. And, as such, whatever makes for the uplift of man is a sacred religious duty to us. Poverty, ignorance, superstition, inertia, the overwhelming sense of helplessness, the absence of legitimate incentive to high social, moral or spiritual effort—all these hinder the realisation of our highest moral and spiritual ideals. In the interest, therefore, of the moral and spiritual life of our nation, we must adopt this policy which is calculated to help the revelation of God in our masses.